Manfred Griehl

Messerschmitt
Aircraft Since 1925

Messerschmitt

Aircraft Since 1925

Manfred Griehl

Pen & Sword
AVIATION

First published in Great Britain in 2015 by
Pen & Sword Aviation
an imprint of
Pen & Sword Books Ltd
47 Church Street
Barnsley
South Yorkshire
S70 2AS

Copyright © Manfred Griehl 2015

ISBN 978 1 78383 169 2

A CIP catalogue record for this book is available from the British Library

Typeset in Ehrhardt by
Mac Style Ltd, Bridlington, East Yorkshire
Printed and bound in Malta by Gutenberg Press

Pen & Sword Books Ltd incorporates the imprints of Pen & Sword Archaeology, Atlas, Aviation, Battleground, Discovery, Family History, History, Maritime, Military, Naval, Politics, Railways, Select, Transport, True Crime, and Fiction, Frontline Books, Leo Cooper, Praetorian Press, Seaforth Publishing and Wharncliffe.

For a complete list of Pen & Sword titles please contact
PEN & SWORD BOOKS LIMITED
47 Church Street, Barnsley, South Yorkshire, S70 2AS, England
E-mail: enquiries@pen-and-sword.co.uk
Website: www.pen-and-sword.co.uk

Photo credits: Photos were provided by the following firms/persons:
Backmann, Borzutzki, Creek, Dabrowski, DAeC, Daimler-Benz Aerospace, EADS, Ewbank, Franzike, Fraport, Griehl, Gros(+), Handig, Herwig(+), Jayne, Jurleit(+), Krieg, Lang, Lange(+), Lommel, Lutz, Mohr(+), Müller, Neitzel, Nowarra(+), Radinger, Rohrbach, Ricco, Schreiber, Selinger, Smith J, Stapfer, Wagner and Werner.

A Brief History of the Manufacturer 7
Acknowledgements 9
Production Data 10
BFW 1 12
BFW 3 13
BFW M-17 14
BFW M-18 a, b, c and d 15
BFW M-19 17
BFW M-20 a, b1 and b2 18
BFW M-21 a and b 20
BFW M-22 21
BFW M-23 a, b and c 22
BFW M-24 a and b 24
BFW M-26 26
BFW M-27 a and b 27
BFW M-28 28
BFW M-29 a and b 29
BFW M-31 31
BFW M-33 32

BFW M-35 a and b 33
BFW M-36 36
BFW M-37/Bf 108 A 37
Bf 108 B-1 to D-1 38
Bf Experimental Aircraft 40
Bf 109 A-0 to B-2 41
Bf 109 C-1 to C-3 42
Bf 109 D-1 43
Bf 109 E-0 to E-9 44
Bf 109 T-1 and T-2 46
Bf 109 with radial motor 47
Bf 109 F-0 to F-6 48
Bf 109 G-0 to G-14 50
Bf 109 H-0 to H-5 53
Bf 109 K-0 to K-14 54
Bf Experimental Aircraft 56
Bf 110 A-0 to B-3 57
Bf 110 C-1 to C-7 58
Bf 110 D-0 to D-4 60

Bf 110 E-1 to E-3 61
Bf 110 F-2 to F-4 62
Bf 110 G-0 to G-4 63
Bf 161 66
Bf 162 67
Bf 163 68
Me 163 A-0 69
Me 163 B-0 to B-2 70
Me 163 C-0 and D-0 72
Me 163 S 73
Me 208 and Nord 1101 74
Me 209 76
Bf (Me) 210 78
Me 261 80
Me Experimental Aircraft 82
Me 262 A-1 83
Me 262 A-1/U4 84
Me 262 A-1/U3 and A-5 85
Me 262 A-2 86
Me 262 B-1 87
Me 262 B-2 (NJ) 88
Me 262 C-1a 89
Me 262 C-2b 90
Me 262 HG I bis III 91
Me 263 (Ju 248) 92
Me 264 94

Me 264/6m 95
Me 309 96
Me 321 A and B 98
Me 323 C 100
Me 323 D-1 to E-1 101
Me 323 E-2 "Weapons Carrier" 104
Me 328 A (Experimental aircraft) 105
Me 328 B (Experimental aircraft) 106
Me 329 107
Me 410 (Experimental aircraft) 108
Me 410 A-1 to A-3 109
Me 410 B-1 to B-8 110
Me P 1100 111
Me P 1101 112
Me P 1106 113
Me P 1110 114
Me P 1112 115
HA 100 116
HA 200 118
HA 300 120
Project 141 122
Project 160 123
Project 308 124
Project 2020 125
VJ 101 A to E 126

Wilhelm Messerschmitt was born on 25 May 1898. It was at the first Frankfurt flying exhibition in the summer of 1909 that his interest in aviation awoke. By September 1914 Messerschmitt was active at Bamberg as an enthusiastic assistant to Friedrich Harth, who had espoused the construction of gliders. In November 1918 he began studying machinery construction at the College for Advanced Technology, Munich. Late in 1921 he built his first glider, the S 10. On 18 September 1922 he revoked his partnership agreement with Harth and in May 1923 at Bamberg founded the Flugzeugbau Messerschmitt. For his engineering diploma, Willy Messerschmitt submitted the design for his S 14 glider. In the following spring he lost interest in gliding and the Rhône competitions and from 1924 turned to the manufacture of motorised light aircraft. He produced seven examples of his first design, the M-17.

On 28 April 1925, also at Bamberg, he founded the limited company Messerschmitt Flugzeugbau GmbH. The Bayrische Flugzeugwerke AG (BFW) was created the same day, and was located subsequently in the hangars of the former Rumpler Works at Augsburg. A workforce of about 400 was employed at the Augsburg Works until December 1930. At the beginning of 1931 the Works encountered grave financial problems. Dornier and Heinkel wanted to take over the company.

The BFW M-17 (D-997) was produced at Bamberg.

The success story of the Messerschmitt Works began with the Bf 109.

The Reich Transport Ministry supported the undertaking, but could not prevent bankruptcy proceedings beginning on 1 June 1931. In March 1933 after Hitler took power Messerschmitt AG received a State contract valued at 1.2 million Reichsmarks which resulted in the bankruptcy proceedings being lifted in August 1933. Shortly afterwards at Messerschmitt a supervisory council was elected, the new chairman being test pilot Theo Croneiss. Willy Messerschmitt, the only board member, became technical director. As from 1934 the former production plant at Augsburg was greatly expanded. A large flight hall was built. Following the successful maiden flights of the Bf 108 A and Bf 109 V1, and also the Bf 110 V1, the former works were rapidly increased in size. The Reich Air Ministry (RLM) made 14 million Reichsmarks available. From 8 May 1937 the BFW Regensburg GmbH at Regensburg served as a further modern plant for the series production of aircraft for the Luftwaffe.

In September 1938, Hermann Göring nominated board member Engineer (Dipl.) Hentzen as a leader of military industry. In March 1939 there was employed in the Augsburg region under his authority a permanent workforce of 6,000 people. Willy Messerschmitt received many honours, being appointed Honourary Professor at Munich and Vice-President of the German Academy for Aviation Research besides other posts. At the factory itself, he had only remained active in the areas of development and construction.

At the outbreak of war, Messerschmitt AG production received a boost in interest from the RLM. Failures such as the Bf 210 resulted in a loss of Willy Messerschmitt's prestige, however. In March 1942 he was summoned to Berlin to report in person. Then, one after another, the maiden flights of the Me 262 with two Jumo 004 jet turbines, of the Me 309 V1, of the Me 328 AV1 and the Me 410 V1 were successful, and also the first flight of the four-engined Me 264. On the other hand, the development of the rocket-fighter, from the Me 163 AV4 to the Me 263 was a less significant episode. As from 1 March 1944 the Armaments Ministry handled all aircraft production in place of the RLM. The

In 1944 the Me 262A revolutionized aerial warfare.

Me 262 A-1a signalled a radical change in aerial armaments in the summer of 1944.

However, the war was lost. On 28 April 1945 US forces arrived at Augsburg and occupied the plant. From 1949 Messerschmitt built prefabricated houses, sewing machines and bubble cars. Collaboration with Spain from 1952 led to the production of the Bf 109 under licence as HA 1109 and Ha 1112. On 30 December 1953 the first aircraft developed by Willy Messerschmitt since the Second World War, the trainer HA 100, made its maiden flight in Spain. The jet HA 200 followed and HA 300 finally built in Egypt.

On 23 February 1959 the work group "Entwicklungsring Süd" (Development Ring South) was founded in which the firms Bölkow, Heinkel and Messerschmitt espoused the development of the vertical take-off aircraft VJ 101. The significant investment resulted in an extremely modern jet aircraft. The West German Air Force decided on a conventional model for operations. US manufacturers were to be awarded the contract. In the end VJ 110 had no chance. From 1966 Willy Messerschmitt interested himself in other development ideas, amongst them vertical take-off transport aircraft such as the "Rotorjet". On 14 May 1968 Messerschmitt-Bölkow-Blohm (MBB) was founded at Ottobrunn. Messerschmitt AG was a holding company in the new firm's structure. Professor Willy Messerschmitt died on 15 September 1978, shortly after his 80th birthday.

An observation in conclusion: because of the extensive material available, only a short impression of Professor Messerschmitt's surprising creations can be provided. Not all types and projects can be put into words and pictures while the numerous gliders also had to be omitted. The same applies also to the development of guided missiles, such as the ground-to-air flak rocket "Enzian".

Acknowledgements

Above all my special thanks got to EADS Deutschland, whose great interest brought to life the products of its predecessors through valuable photographic material. Deutsche Lufthansa, Flughafen AG Frankfurt (Fraport) and BMW Munich also contributed to this production. Many of the photos were provided selflessly by Hans-Peter Dabrowski, the late Wernfried Haberfellner, the late Theodor Mohr, Willy Radinger, Franz Selinger and friends from England, France, Austria and the United States. Without their help this chronicle of the Messerschmitt aircraft types would not have been so fascinating.

The HA 100 was built in Spain.

As a rule, Messerschmitt aircraft up to the M-36 were turned out in small quantities. Only the BFW M-20, M-23 and M-35 proved more successful. Production numbers rose after rearmament began and the German air arm came into being. This was true particularly in the cases of the Bf 109, Bf 110, Me 163, Bf 210, Me 262 and Me 410.

BFW Series: 1 "Sperber" – 1: 3a/b "Marabu" – 1: M-17 "Ello" – 7: M-18 a to d – 8: M-19 – 2: M-20 a to b2 – 12: M-21 a and b – 2: M-22 – 1: M-23 a to c – 70: M-24 a and b – 2: M-26 a – 1: M-27 a and b – 3: M-28 – 1: M-29 a and b – 6: M-31 – 1: M-35 a and b – 15: M-36 – 5.

Bf Series: 108 – 955: 109 – 33,675: 110 – 5960: 161 – 2: 162 – 3: 163 – 1.

Me Series: 163 – 485: 208 – 2: 209 – 4: 210 – 480 (some converted to Me 410): 261 – 3: 262 – 1433: 263 – 1: 264 – 1: 309 – 4: 321 – 201 (some converted to Me 323): 323 – 198: 328 – 5 (some converted): 410 – 1015: P 1101 – 1 (under construction in 1945).

NB: The production figures vary to some extent depending on the sources and have been taken, as far as possible, from the available original files.

Above: Series production of the Bf 109 G-3 fighter.

Below: Production of the Me 262 A-1a in one of the "forest factories".

BFW 1 "Sperber"

This first own-construction of the Bavarian
Aircraft Works (BFW) was based on Udet's
U-12b. It was a two-seat trainer of mixed-
method development, propulsion being
provided by a Siemens-Halske Sh-12 radial
motor. The fuselage was a steel tube with fabric
covering. Only one prototype (Works Nr. 351,
D-1315) was built: it was flown from 1927 by
DVL. In February 1928 the well-known aviator
Alexander von Bismarck obtained the machine
for aerial acrobatic displays. In October 1929
Eugen, Prince of Schaumburg-Lippe, took the
aircraft over. It flew until last heard of in August
1931.

Aircraft Type:	BFW 1
Purpose:	Trainer
Crew:	Two
Engine plant:	1 x Siemens-Halske Sh 12 (92 kW, 125 hp)
Wingspan:	10 metres
Length:	7.4 m
Height:	2.78 m
Wing area:	26.5 m2
Top speed:	137 km/hr
Cruising speed:	110 kms/hr
Landing speed:	75 kms/hr
Rate of climb to 2,000 metres:	20 mins
Weight empty:	600 kgs
All-up weight:	900 kgs
Service ceiling:	3,600 m
Range:	400 kms

*The BFW S-1 "Sperber" had good flight
characteristics.*

BFW3 a and 3b "Marabu"

The BFW 3a was intended primarily as a two-seat biplane trainer for flying schools. Like the FW 1 the design was based on the Udet-12b with a mixed method of construction. Only one model of the BFW 3a (Works Nr. 352, D-925) was built due to financial constraints. The machine first flew in 1927, received its licence in February 1927 and operated in 1928 at BFW Augsburg. Propulsion was a Siemens-Halske Sh 11 motor. In June 1928 the "Marabu" was sold to the Deutsche Verkehrsfliegerschule GmbH (German Commercial Flying School) and flew in the Königsberg area from August that year. As to the subsequent whereabouts of the aircraft nothing is known. The BFW 3b with a more efficient engine remained on the drawing board.

Aircraft Type:	BFW 3a
Purpose:	Trainer
Crew:	Two
Engine plant:	1 x Siemens-Halske Sh 11 (82 kW, 112 hp)
Wingspan:	10 m
Length:	7.5 m
Height:	2.63 m
Wing area:	24 m²
Top speed:	136 kms/hr
Cruising speed:	105 kms/hr
Landing speed:	75 kms/hr
Rate of climb to 1,000 metres:	11 mins
Weight empty:	530 kg
All-up weight:	800 kgs
Service ceiling:	3,300 m
Range:	500 m

The BFW S-3a bore a great similarity to the Udet U12a.

BFW M-17

The light two-seater M-17, a further development of the motor-glider S-16b, was the first "pure" motorised aircraft produced by Willy Messerschmitt. It was a wooden-built monoplane with an unbraced high wing intended to train civilian pilots for German commercial air operations under development in the mid-1920s. The prototype (Works Nr. 20) resulted from a conversion of the S-16b at Bamberg in the autumn of 1925 fitted with a 700 cubic metre Douglas motor. It was expected to take part in the Zugspitze competition that year but nothing came of this. Subsequently six machines (Work Nrs. 21 to 26) were manufactured with various motor installations. After the ABC "Scorpion", the last two training machines had a Bristol "Cherub" engine. Theo Croneiss used machine Work Nr. 25 to win several prizes in 1925. The M-17 was considered by the DVL at Berlin-Staaken as the best motorised aircraft since the end of the World War.

Aircraft Type:	BFW M-17
Purpose:	Training and Sport
Crew:	One or two
Engine plant:	1 x ABC Scorpion (18 kW, 24 hp) or Bristol Cherub (24 kW, 32 hp)
Wingspan:	11.6 m
Length:	5.85 m
Height:	1.8 m
Wing area:	10.4 sq.m
Top speed:	132 kms/hr
Cruising speed:	115 kms/hr
Landing speed:	68 kms/hr
Rate of climb to 1,000 metres:	9.6 mins
Weight empty:	186 kg
All-up weight:	370 kgs
Service ceiling:	4,000 m
Range:	not known

The M-18 a (centre) and two BFW M-17s being prepared for flight.

Motor Aircraft M-18 a, b, c, and d

The four-seater BFW M-18 carried three passengers and was intended as a feeder for the commercial airlines. Dating from the autumn of 1925, it was the first metal-built aircraft to be manufactured by Messerschmitt. Initially a Siemens Halske Sh 11 of 59 kW (80 hp) was installed. Theo Croneiss piloted the machine (D-947) on its maiden flight on 15 June 1926. The second of the series, the M-18b (D-1118) had capacity for four passengers and was fitted with a more efficient Sh12 motor of 74 kW (100 hp) in 1927. Another four aircraft of the type were turned out at Bamberg and production continued at Augsburg after the relocation there. The M-18b produced at Augsburg became the standard version.

Aircraft Type:	M-18 d
Purpose:	Commercial and Photo Aircraft
Crew:	One
Engine plant:	1 x Wright 300 (231 kW, 315 hp)
Wingspan:	15.8 m
Length:	9 m
Height:	2.7 m
Wing area:	25.4 sq. m
Top speed:	212 kms/hr
Cruising speed:	165 kms/hr
Landing speed:	85 kms/hr
Rate of climb to 3,000 metres:	21.5 mins
Weight empty:	870 kgs
All-up weight:	1760 kgs
Service ceiling:	5,000 m
Range:	800 kms

The BFW M-18 flew principally with Verkehrsflug AG of northern Bavaria.

The M-18 c of 1929, fitted with several seats and used for aerial photography, was propelled by an Armstrong-Siddely "Lynx" 162 kW (220 hp) engine. Most machines of this version were flown by Nordbayrischer Verkehrsflug AG. Messerschmitt used an M-18 c as the firm's machine in 1929. The various commercial and photography aircraft M-18 d had either an Armstrong-Siddely "Lynx", a Walter "Mars" or a Wright "Whirlwind" engine and were also used abroad. In the winter of 1933 an M-20 d (D-ORIZ) was fitted with an As 10 c inverted inline motor.

Side view of the BFW M-18 c as the BFW firm's aircraft.

The BFW M-18 d was used occasionally as a floatplane.

BFW M-19

The single-seat wooden-built low-wing sporting monoplane BFW M-19 (D-1206, Works Nr. 31) was built specially by Willy Messerschmitt for the Sachsenflug (Saxony Aerial Competition) of 1927. The machine was equipped with a Bristol "Cherub" 21 kW motor (28 hp) replaced later with a more powerful 26 kW (36 hp) version. The second model (D-1221, Works Nr 35) appeared in the spring of 1927. Both machines competed in the Sachsenflug. D-1206 piloted by E. von Conta crashed on the final stretch but was awarded second place in the overall assessment. D-1221 was flown by Theo Croneiss in the competition and qualified. It was later piloted by Werner von Langsdorff. The machine broke up after hitting a tree near Augsburg aerodrome on 8 August 1945 as a result of pilot error. The M-19 was the direct predecessor of the two-seater BFW M-23.

Aircraft Type:	BFW M-19
Purpose:	Sporting aircraft
Crew:	One
Engine plant:	1 x Bristol "Cherub" (26 kW, 36 hp)
Wingspan:	9.6 m
Length:	5.4 m
Height:	1.5 m
Wing area:	7.9 sq.m
Top speed:	115 kms/hr
Cruising speed:	80 kms/hr
Landing speed:	65 kms/hr
Rate of climb to 1,000 metres:	8 mins
Weight empty:	158 kgs
All-up weight:	336 kgs
Service ceiling:	800 m
Range:	Not known

The BFW M-19 was the fore-runner of the M-23.

BFW M-20 a, b1 and b2

Aircraft Type:	BFW M-20 b1
Purpose:	Commercial aircraft
Crew:	Two
Passengers:	Ten to twelve
Engine plant:	1 x BMW V1 NZ 500 (470 kW 640 hp)
Wingspan:	26.5 m
Length:	15.8 m
Height:	4.8 m
Wing area:	73.8 sq.m
Top speed:	205 kms/hr
Cruising speed:	155 kms/hr
Landing speed:	85 kms/hr
Rate of climb to 3,000 metres:	25 mins
Weight empty:	2990 kgs
All-up weight:	4800 kgs
Service ceiling:	5400 m
Range:	550 kms

Still at Bamberg, Messerschmitt proceeded with his concept of a large aircraft of all-metal construction, the M-20. His design arose from the desire for a commercial machine with ten passengers' capacity. "Deutsche Luft Hansa" of the time ordered two versions for trials (M-20 a). The first of these crashed on its maiden flight on 26 February 1928. Although the order was revoked, BFW completed the second machine then under construction. After this flew successfully on 3 August 1928 Deutsche Luft Hansa ordered two variants with the BMW V1 5.5Z (max. 515 kW, 700 hp) more powerful engine plant. The two aircraft were accepted by Deutsche Luft Hansa in the summer of 1929

The BFW M-20 a (Works Nr. 421, D-1676) bore the name "Schwaben".

under the designation M-20 b1. As the result of two crashes in 1930 and 1931, the production of the M-20 b2 was halted when it was discovered that the weight capacity in the specifications was mis-stated. Although Erhard Milch then cancelled the order for ten M-20 b2's, the firm went through with the project and the aircraft later proved very safe.

The BFW M-20 was fitted with various engine plants.

The BFW M-20 b (Works Nr. 545 D-2290) flew between 1932 and 1937.

BFW M-21 a and b

The M-21 biplane was ordered by the Reich Transport Ministry (RVM) in two variants as a two-seater trainer for the commercial flying school. The difference between the two was the engine plant, this being a Siemens-Halske Sh 11 of 59 kW (80 hp) for the M-21 a and an Sh 12 of 74 kW (100 hp) for the M-21 b. Unlike most other training machines the M-21 had a tubular steel fuselage instead of plywood. The design allowed for folding wings. The two prototypes were tried out by Theo Croneiss from 17 August 1928. Although the performance was about 10 per cent higher than in comparable aircraft no series contract was forthcoming. Later the two prototypes went to the DVS where they were frequently used with skis.

Aircraft Type:	BFW M-21 b
Purpose:	Trainer
Crew:	Two
Engine plant:	1 x Siemens-Halske Sh 12 (74 kW 100 hp)
Wingspan:	10 m
Length:	7.2 m
Height:	2.8 m
Wing area:	20.8 sq.m
Top speed:	156 kms/hr
Cruising speed:	40 km/hr
Landing speed:	75 kms/hr
Rate of climb to 1,000 metres:	7 mins
Weight empty:	480 kgs
All-up weight:	740 kgs
Service ceiling:	3,800 m
Range:	600 kms

The undercarriage of the sporting aircraft BFW M-21 (D-1525) was fitted with skis.

BFW M-22

The "twin-engined biplane" M-22 was produced in a mixture of tubular steel and wood and driven by two Siemens "Jupiter" motors. It was principally a night bomber and reconnaissance machine which could also serve as a night fighter should circumstances require it. The development began in 1929. Works pilot Franz Sido flew the only prototype for the first time in April 1930. On 6 May that year during a night flight the machine crashed with substantial damage. After repairs, trials continued. The machine was taken over by the Reichswehr on 14 October 1930. Flown by Reichswehr pilot Eberhard Mohnike it crashed into a wood near Augsburg aerodrome. The enquiry established that the pilot had attempted to loop the loop, which was not an approved manoeuvre, resulting in one of the three-bladed propellors breaking, depriving the pilot of control.

Aircraft Type:	BFW M-22
Purpose:	Bomber for night operations
Crew:	Two to three
Engine plant:	2 x Siemens Jupiter (2 x 368 kW, 2 x 500 hp)
Wingspan:	17 m
Length:	13.6 m
Height:	4.8 m
Wing area:	63.2 sq.m
Top speed:	220 kms/hr
Cruising speed:	185 kms/hr
Landing speed:	95 kms/hr
Rate of climb to 3,000 metres:	8.5.mins
Weight empty:	2900 kgs
All-up weight:	3800 kgs
Service ceiling:	6200 m
Range:	500 kms, no armament

The Reichswehr lost interest in the BFW M-22 bomber.

BFW M23 a, b and c

The single-engined low wing monoplane BFW M-23 was developed at the end of 1928 based on the discontinued M-19. The first version, the M-23 a (Works Nr 418) was fitted with an ABC "Scorpion" motor and shown to the ILA in October 1928. The next two machines had either a "Salmson" motor or an Armstrong-Siddeley "Genet" (D-1571). The series ran to only nine machines. The fuselage framework of the M-20b was altered to allow for reinforcement and a larger rudder. Work on the first M-20 b (Works Nr 449) was begun in September 1928 and the machine was first flown in March 1929. Engine plant was an Sh 13 of 66 kW (90 hp). It flew successfully in the Round-Europe competition of 1929. By the end of 1931 a total of 70 M-20 b's had been turned out. In 1930 an experimental M-20 b with an Sh 13 engine was equipped with two floats. The M-20 c was prepared for the international competition of 1930; the M-20 c flown by Fritz Morzik won.

Aircraft Type:	BFW M-23 c
Purpose:	Training and sporting aircraft
Crew:	Two
Engine plant:	1 x Argus As 8 (74 kW, 100 hp)
Wingspan:	12 m
Length:	7.4 m
Height:	4.2 m
Wing area:	14.3 sq.m
Top speed:	220 kms/hr
Cruising speed:	185 kms/hr
Landing speed:	64 kms/hr
Rate of climb to 3,000 m:	16 mins
Weight empty:	280 kgs
All-up weight:	600 kgs
Service ceiling:	6200 m
Range:	750 kms

The BFW M-23 a on the airfield at Augsburg.

Designation M-23 b W was used as a light floatplane.

The BFW M-23c model was racy when fitted with an inverted inline engine.

BFW M-24 a and b

Ever larger aircraft were required for the increase in air travel. The development of the commercial airliner M-24 began in 1928. This was a machine for eight passengers or 1000 kgs cargo. The prototype M-24 a (D-1767 Works Nr. 445) was designed for a Jumo L-5G or a BMW Va, and manufactured to the usual Dural all-metal technique. The high wing surface passed through the upper fuselage. The maiden flight equipped with the BMW Va was made by Theo Croneiss on 8 July 1929, the aircraft then going to the Nordbayrische Verkehrsflug AG, the second in May 1930 to the DVL at Berlin-Adlershof. Two further M-24 a's followed. These

Aircraft Type:	BFW M-24 b
Purpose:	Passengers and cargo
Crew:	Two
Passenger:	Six to eight
Engine plant:	1 x Siemens Jupiter (254-368 kW, 346-500 hp)
Wingspan:	30.4 m
Length:	12.8 m
Height:	3.2 m
Wing area:	43 sq.m
Top speed:	220 kms/hr
Cruising speed:	190 kms/hr
Landing speed:	82 kms/hr
Rate of climb to 3000 m:	15 mins
Weight empty:	1630 kgs
All-up weight:	2900 kgs
Service ceiling:	5000 m
Range:	780 kms.

Sales of the BFW M-24 were modest.

aircraft (Works Nrs. 515 and 516) had more powerful BMW Hornet motors and a larger rudder unit. The first of them received a Siemens Jupiter radial engine (320 kW, 435 hp) and was tried out with floats at Travemünde in 1932. The Reich Air Ministry (RLM) took over the second.

The BFW M-24 W was operated by the firm Bayernflug of Augsburg.

BFW M-26 a

The high-speed M-26 was designed for two passengers. Work on the all-metal high wing aircraft began in 1929. Messerschmitt chose a Siemens-Halske radial motor for the engine plant. Two M-26 a's were ordered but only the first (D-2085 Works Nr 483) was built, and was flown successfully in October 1929 by Works pilot Sido. Further work on this design stalled after the US partner organisation Eastern Aircraft Corporation became a victim of the world economic crisis. Following a spell as the firm's aircraft, the single M-26 a was taken over a few years later by the RLM. Only components of the second model remained after the design was abandoned. The more powerful Sh 14 engine was therefore never produced.

Aircraft Type:	BFW M-26
Purpose:	High-speed aircraft
Crew:	One
Passengers:	Two
Engine plant:	1 x Siemens-Halske Sh 11 or 12 (68-74 kW, 92-100 hp)
Wingspan:	12.4 m
Length:	7.15 m
Height:	2.3 m
Wing area:	14.3 sq.m
Top speed:	170 kms/hr
Cruising speed:	142 kms/hr
Landing speed:	85 kms/hr
Rate of climb to 2,000 m:	14 mins
Weight empty:	460 kgs
All-up weight:	960 kgs
Service ceiling:	3700 m
Range:	850 kms

The BFW M-26 was designed as a three-seater small commercial aircraft.

BFW M-27 a and b

The two-seater M-27 was a sport and training low-wing monoplane based on the proven M-23. Of mixed construction materials, the fitting of a powerful inverted-V engine made the machine suitable for flying schools. The prototype M-27 a (D-1979, Works Nr. 539) therefore received an air-cooled Argus As 8. The machine had a narrow wing to ensure airflow in the rudder area. The experimental machine flew for the first time in July 1931. Theo Corneiss piloted it in August that year in the Germany competition but was forced to drop out early on with engine damage. The other M-27 a's (Works Nrs. 609 and 610) were both lost in flat tailspin crashes. Works pilot Willi Stör parachuted free both times. Another nine M-27's were produced between June 1933 and February 1934, of these the machines fitted with the Argus As 8R were designated M-27 b.

Aircraft Type:	BFW M-27 a and b
Purpose:	Trainer
Crew:	Two
Engine plant:	1 x Arggus AS 8 or As 8R (92-110 kW, 125-150 hp)
Wingspan:	12 m
Length:	7.9 m
Height:	2.4 m
Wing area:	14.5 sq.m
Top speed:	200 kms/hr
Cruising speed:	170 kms/hr
Landing speed:	75 kms/hr
Rate of climb to 3000 m:	17.3 mins
Weight empty:	420 kgs
All-up weight:	720 kgs
Service ceiling:	5200 m
Range:	700 kms

The two-seater BFW M-27 flew as a two-seater sports aircraft.

BFW M-28

As the demand for airmail services became greater, Deutsche Luft Hansa, which operated the routes for the Reichspost, began looking for a fast mail-carrier. Messerschmitt thus conceived the M-28 as a high wing aircraft along the lines of the M-20/M-24. The only machine finally completed (D-2059, Works Nr. 527) was given a nine-cylinder BM Hornet radial motor. Works pilot Franz Sido made the maiden flight in February 1931. The two-seater was all metal except for parts of the wing and rudder. The two crew sat side by side in the roomy cabin adjacent to a large cargo hold. It soon became obvious that this kind of purpose-built aircraft was not the best solution, and the machine was later passed to the DVL in Berlin-Adlershof where it was used for resistance testing from 1932.

Aircraft Type:	BFW M-28
Purpose:	Fast mail carrier
Crew:	Two
Engine plant:	1 x BMW Hornet (386 kW, 525 hp)
Wingspan:	15.5 m
Length:	10 m
Height:	3 m
Wing area:	25.6 sq.m
Top speed:	260 kms/hr
Cruising speed:	220 kms/hr
Landing speed:	90 kms/hr
Rate of climb to 3000 m:	12 minutes
Weight empty:	1160 kg
All-up weight:	2570 kgs
Service ceiling:	5200 kms
Range:	2500 kms

The postal aircraft BFW M-28 was unwanted by the market.

BFW M-29 a and b

In 1931 the Messerschmitt Works received from the Reich Air Ministry an invitation to tender for a two-seater to take part in the Round-Europe Competition of 1932. The M-29 was designed as a high-wing cabin dual-seater of mixed construction materials. A novelty of the design were landing flaps and a self-aligning rudder designed by Willy Messerschmitt. The first of six M-29's (Works Nr. 601) were flown on 13 April 1932 by Works pilot Erwin Eichele. Engine plant was an Argus As 8R inverted-V motor. The second model (Works Nr 602, D-2306) received

Aircraft Type:	BFW M-29
Purpose:	Sport aicraft for Round-Europe Competition
Crew:	Two
Engine plant:	1 x Argus As 8R (92-110 kW, 125–150 hp)
Wingspan:	10.8 m
Length:	7.75 m
Height:	2 m
Wing area:	14.4 sq.m
Top speed:	260 kms/hr
Cruising speed:	225 kms/hr
Landing speed:	65 kms/hr
Rate of climb to 3000 m:	11 mins
Weight empty:	400 kgs
All-up weight:	700 kgs
Service ceiling:	6000 m
Range:	700 kms

The wings of the BFW M-29 could be folded back.

a Siemens-Halske Sh 14 radial motor. After two M-29's crashed in August 1932, the M-29 was grounded and the third aircraft (Works Nr. 603, D-2307) was therefore excluded from the Competition. After faults in the elevator unit were corrected three more machines of the type were built and fitted with the Argus engine.

The BFW M-29 a was clear to fly in the spring of 1932.

The BFW M-29 b had a Siemens-Halske radial motor.

BFW M-31

The two-seater M-31 was planned as a more economically priced yet thoroughly robust machine compared to other sports and training aircraft available hitherto. The M-31 (Works Nr 607, D-2623) was an unbraced low wing monoplane of mixed construction materials with wooden wings in trapezoid configuration and steel tubular fuselage. The only prototype was put on show at the 1932 German Aviation Exhibition in Berlin. Engine plant was initially a light BMW Xa radial motor. Erwin Aichele made the maiden flight at the beginning of August 1932. Performance in flight failed to match up to requirements, and the original engine was replaced by the more efficient Hirth HM 60 inverted-V motor. The market was not interested in the machine, which was taken over by the RLM in 1933.

Aircraft Type:	BFW M-31
Purpose:	Sport and trainer
Crew:	Two
Engine plant:	1 x Hirth HM 60 (48-51 kW, 65–70 hp)
Wingspan:	12 m
Length:	7.85 m
Height:	1.9 m
Wing area:	17 sq.m
Top speed:	170 kms/hr
Cruising speed:	140 kms/hr
Landing speed:	70 kms/hr
Rate of climb to 3000 m:	27 mins
Weight empty:	335 kgs
All-up weight:	650 kgs
Service ceiling:	3800 m
Range:	700 m

The two-seater BFW M-31 was taken over by the Reich Air Ministry.

BFW M-33

Aircraft Type:	BFW M-33
Purpose:	"The People's Aircraft"
Crew:	One
Engine plant:	1 x DKW Type 6 (11 kW, 15 hp)
Wingspan:	9.26 m
Length:	5.65 m
Height:	1.95 m, no other information as to wing area, speeds, rate of climb, empty and maximum take-off weights, ceiling or range are known.

The M-33 was first displayed at the German Aviation Exhibition DELA in 1932 as the full-size mock-up of a construction set aircraft. The small single-seater was to have had a light DKW type P-motor. Only the fuselage frame with prefabricated socket for the motor, diverse mounts and fittings for the wings and control components were to be supplied, the remainder was to be built by the purchaser to the plans. The midget aircraft was designed primarily for aviation clubs which would have suitable facilities for the building work. As conventional construction models were superior, the DIY aircraft was consigned to the archives.

BFW M-35 a and b

The M-35 of mixed construction materials was based on the M-31 but of far higher performance. It was an unbraced low wing monoplane equally useful for training and stunt flying with stowage in the wings for packs. The wings and control surfaces were of wood/metal materials, the fuselage a steel tube construction. The M-35 was the last sports aircraft initiated by Willy Messerschmitt. The first two prototypes, the single-seater M-35 a (Works Nr. 620) and the two- seater M-35 b with dual controls (Works Nr 621) were ready by the summer of 1933. Works pilot Aichele made the maiden flights. Only two of the 14 M-35 b were fitted with an Argus As 17A inverted-V motor, the others and the M-35 a had an Sh 14 engine plant. The aircraft were delivered in the period from March 1934 to September 1935. The last machine of the series, a single seater aerobatics aircraft, the M-35 b (Works Nr. 646, D-EQAN) went to Will Stör who used it to become aerobatics world champion in 1935 and 1936.

Aircraft Type:	BFW M-35 b
Purpose:	Trainer and sports aircraft
Crew:	Two
Engine plant:	1 x Siemens-Halske Sh 14 (110 kW, 150 hp)
Wingspan:	11.57 m
Length:	7.42 m
Height:	2.75 m
Wing area:	17 sq.m
Top speed:	230 kms/hr
Cruising speed:	205 kms/hr
Landing speed:	75 kms/hr
Rate of climb to 3,000 m:	14.8 mins
Weight empty:	500 kgs
All-up weight:	810 kgs
Service ceiling:	5300 m
Range:	700 m

The dual seater trainer BFW M-35 b was built until 1935.

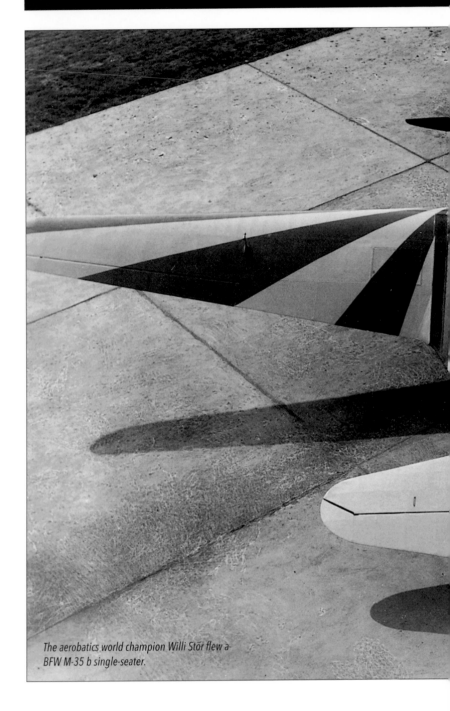

The aerobatics world champion Willi Stör flew a BFW M-35 b single-seater.

BFW M-36/ICAR "Comercial"

The BFW M-36 was a passenger aircraft built for Romania, designed in Augsburg and manufactured in Bucharest at Intrepindere Pentru Constructi Aeronautice Romane (ICAR). The concept was a robust, single-engined high wing monoplane with a well covered landing gear using mixed materials. The fuselage had room for two crew and six passengers. A Gnome & Rhone K-14 engine was originally planned, but the Romanians preferred the weaker Armstrong-Siddeley Serval Mk.1 which provided only 265 kW (360 hp) as against the original 335 kW (455 hp). The test flights in Romania at the end of 1934 with the YR-ACS proved very successful. Several machines of the type flew between 1936 and 1938 for the national airline LARES.

Aircraft Type:	BFW M-36
Purpose:	Commercial airliner
Crew:	Two
Passengers:	Six
Engine plant:	1 x Armstrong Siddeley Serv Mk.1 (265 kW, 360 hp)
Wingspan:	10.31 m
Length:	8.06 m
Height:	2.02 m
Wing area:	16 sq.m
Top speed:	300 kms/hr
Cruising speed:	250 kms/hr
Landing speed:	65 kms/hr
Rate of climb to 1000 m:	3.15 mins
Weight empty:	560 kgs
All-up weight:	1015 kgs
Service ceiling:	6500 m
Range:	700 kms

The joint BFW/ICAR production M-36 was used as a passenger aircraft in Rumania.

BFW M-37 a and Bf 108 a "Taifun"

Aircraft Type:	BFW M-37 a and Bf 108 a
Purpose:	Tourer
Crew:	One or two
Passengers:	One to three
Engine plant:	1 x Hirth HM 8U (177 kW, 240 hp)
Wingspan:	10.31 m
Length:	8.06 m
Height:	2.02 m
Wing area:	16 sq.m
Top speed:	300 kms/hr
Cruising speed:	250 kms/hr
Landing speed:	65 kms/hr
Rate of climb to 1000 m:	3.15 mins
Weight empty:	560 kgs
All-up weight:	1050 kgs
Service ceiling:	6500 m
Range:	700 kms

In June 1933 the Reich Air Ministry invited designs for a four-seater tourer aircraft specially for the Round-Europe Competition of 1934. The work was initially designated M-37 a at Messerschmitt internally, but on the first flight on 13 June 1934 the machine was known as the Bf 108 A V1 (Works Nr 695, D-IBUM). Pilot of this unique version with wooden wings was Carl Francke. All aircraft from Bf 108 A V2 onward received smooth metal skin shell-wings provided with state-of-the-art leading edge slats and large Fowler landing flaps. The wings could be folded back easily against the fuselage. The first Bf 108's had a Hirth HM 8 U engine, an Argus 10C inverted-V motor being fitted to some models later. During a test flight of the prototype V1 to check the slow speed characteristics of the aircraft contact was made involuntarily with the ground, killing the RLM pilot Baron Wolf von Dungern. Bf 108 V7 was fitted with the Sh 14 A-4. Major Seidemann took the experimental version D-IELE on the radial flight at the 1936 Winter Olympics.

A Bf 108 "Taifun" over the Alps.

Bf 108 B to D

In January 1935 Messerschmitt received an invitation to submit his design for a three-seater tourist aircraft with inverted-V engine. The former A configuration was reworked extensively and fitted with an Argus As 10C-1 engine, with variable pitch propellor, automatic leading edge slats and larger wingspan. The prototype fitted with the Argus As 10 C3 from June 1936 was the Bf 108 B V7 (Works Nr 877). This was followed by a nil series of at least four Bf 109 B-0's. The subsequent B-1 series contained a variant B-1s with blind-flying facility. The first purely military version was the Bf 108 B-2. The Bf 108 C-1 (Works Nr. 1078, D-IAXC) had an HM 508C engine enabling it to reach an altitude of 9075 m. Only two of these

Aircraft Type:	Bf 108 D-1
Purpose:	Communications aircraft
Crew:	One to three
Engine plant:	1 x Argus As 10 C (177 kW, 240 hp)
Wingspan:	10.62 m
Length:	8.3 m
Height:	2.02 m
Wing area:	16.4 sq.m
Top speed:	305 kms/hr
Cruising speed:	265 kms/hr
Landing speed:	65 kms/hr
Rate of climb to 1000 m:	3.1 mins
Weight empty:	880 kg
All-up weight:	1380 kgs
Service ceiling:	5000 m
Range:	980 kms

Friedrich Christiansen landed at Frankfurt on 31 July 1938 with this Bf 108.

machines were manufactured. The only three-seater version Bf 108 D-1 was built specially for the Luftwaffe as a communications and liaison aircraft. The machine was noted for its improved rudder unit. From this series and also the B-1, variants suitable for the tropics (B-1/trop. and D-1/trop.) were forthcoming. Production of the Bf 108 B continued at Augsburg until the autumn of 1936 when transferred to Regensburg. From the autumn of 1941 the D-1 version was built in considerable numbers in France. The Bf 108 was exported to numerous buyers overseas including Bulgaria, Japan, Hungary, the United States and Sweden. On the other hand Messerschmitt had no luck with his six seater Me 108F project in 1975.

The functional cabin of a Bf 108 "Taifun".

Bf 109 Experimental Aircraft

Aircraft Type:	Bf 109 V 1
Purpose:	Experimental aircraft (light fighter)
Crew:	One
Engine plant:	1 x Rolls-Royce Kestrel Mk II (429 kW, 583 hp)
Wingspan:	9.89 m
Length:	8.88 m
Height:	2.45 m
Wing area:	16 sq.m
Top speed:	446 kms/hr
Cruising speed:	350 kms/hr
Landing speed:	110 kms/hr
Rate of climb to 5000 m:	7.5 mins
Weight empty:	1400 kgs
All-up weight:	1800 kgs
Service ceiling:	6000+ m
Range:	440 kms
Armament:	none

The RLM development requirement for a "fast pursuit fighter" (VJ) was in Messerschmitt's hands by December 1933. In the spring of 1936 questions of detail such as the future engine plant and armament were discussed. Initially, principally Jumo 10 (210) and also the BMW 116 motor were planned. Armament was to be either an MG C/30 firing through the propellor hub, two MG 17s firing through the propellor circle or two of these weapons and an MG FF on a motorised mounting. The aircraft was to be an all-metal unbraced low wing monoplane in Schalenbauweise. Construction of the prototype began in August 1934. The Bf 109 V-1 (Works Nr 758 D-IABI), the first experimental model, was given a Rolls-Royce Kestrel Mk II motor. The prototype was followed by more than thirty further experimental machines (V-2 to V-30) as well as the prototype for the high altitude fighter version (V-49 to V-55). Corresponding series aircraft were built to test the Bf 109 G and K.

The first experimental Bf 109 from which over 30,000 such machines would ensue.

Bf 109 A-0, A-1, B-0 to B-2

The Bf 109 was intended to replace the existing Ar 68 and He 51 fighters. Only about 20 units of the Bf 109 A-0 and A-1 series were built, some armed with the MG C/30 which fired through the motor hub. Bf 109 V-12 (Works Nr. 1016) was tested with two MG FF in the wings and two MG 17 in the fuselage. These machines all had a Jumo 210D motor. As the introduction of motor hub-gun was not expected to proceed at that time, the series ran to completion with the B version. The Bf 109 B-0 was considered a "light fighter" with Jumo 210 engines and mostly two MG 17s. Bf 109 V-4 to V-11 and V-15 served as the prototypes. The later machines of the series (B-1) had a Jumo 210 with rigid wooden propellor. The fighters had a fixed armament of three MGs installed in the fuselage. Adjustable propellors were fitted to the B-2 version, this being the

Aircraft Type:	Bf 109 B-1
Purpose:	Single seater fighter
Crew:	One
Engine plant:	1 x Juno 210D (500 kW, 680 hp)
Wingspan:	9.9 m
Length:	8.7 m
Height:	2.45 m
Wing area:	16 sq.m
Top speed:	460 kms/hr/ 446 kms/hr (low level)
Landing speed:	105 kms/hr
Rate of climb to 6000 m:	6.8 mins
Weight empty:	1430 kgs
All-up weight:	1955 kgs
Service ceiling:	8000 m
Range:	450 kms
Armament:	3 x MG 17 (through motor hub and wings)

only difference from the B-1. 39 B-1s and B-2s were operational in Spain during the civil war. Because the armament proved too weak and the range was modest, the Luftwaffe decided for the Bf 109 C.

The performance of the Bf 109 B did not satisfy the Luftwaffe for long.

Bf 109 C-1 to C-3 "Caesar"

Aircraft Type:	Bf 109 C-1
Purpose:	Single seater fighter
Crew:	One
Engine plant:	1 x Jumo 210G (508-537 kW, 690-730 hp)
Wingspan:	9.9 m
Length:	8.7 m
Height:	2.5 m
Wing area:	16.4 sq.m
Top speed:	498 kms/hr at 5000 metres altitude
Cruising speed:	(low level) 436 kms/hr
Landing speed:	111 kms/hr
Rate of climb to 5000 m:	7.1 mins
Weight empty:	1523 kgs
All-up weight:	2160 kgs
Service ceiling:	9000 m
Range:	450 kms
Armament:	2 x MG 17 (fuselage) and 2 x MG 17 (wings)

As a result of the tactical experience gained in Spain, the next series Bf 109 C-1 received the more powerful Jumo 210 G engine with variable pitch VDM airscrew. The fuselage fuel tank was enlarged by 102 litres to 357 litres to increase the range. In general, armament consisted of four MG 17s in the fuselage and wings. 58 C-1's were turned out at the Augsburg Works. Apart from the prototype, the variant Bf 109 C-2 series with an MG FF in the fuselage was not proceeded with as a result of problems with the motor-cannon. The next version was therefore the Bf 109 C-3. This was to have two MG FF in the wings along with the previous fuselage armament of two MG 17s, but only a few prototypes were built. The Bf 109 C-3 basically served to close the gap until the Bf 109 E with MG FF-armament became available.

This BF 109 C (SW+EN) came to grief at the Wiener Neustadt works.

Bf 109 D-1 "Dora"

Many more Bf 109 D-1 machines were built than the C-1. This came about because the Jumo 210 Da inverted-V motors which had become available meanwhile were more reliable. The armament of the new version was only four MGs in the fuselage and wings. The MG FF was not one of them. The radio equipment and fuel installation was as for the C-1. The D-1 wing caps strongly resembled those of the Bf 109 E then under development. Performance of the Jumo 210 Da did not match up to the DB 601. Due to delays in development of this motor, it was first used with the Bf 109 E. 36 Bf 109 D aircraft were delivered to Spain during the civil war and flown as fighters or fighter-bombers by the Legion Condor. Switzerland received five in 1938/39. The machine was only rarely seen operating over Poland.

Aircraft Type:	Bf 109 D-1
Purpose:	One-seater fighter
Crew:	One
Engine plant:	1 x Jumo 210Da (412-537 kW, 560-739 hp)
Wingspan:	9.9 m
Length:	8.7 m
Height:	2.5 m
Wing area:	16.4 sq.m
Top speed:	471 kms/hr at 5000 m
Cruising speed:	435 kms/hr (low level)
Landing speed:	111 kms/hr
Rate of climb to 5000 m:	7.1 mins
Weight empty:	1523 kgs
All-up weight:	2160 kgs
Service ceiling:	8000 m
Range:	450 kms
Armament:	4 x MG 17 (fuselage and wings)

Large numbers of the BF 109 D were to be found in pilot training schools at the end of the 1930s.

Bf 109 E-0 to E-9 "Emil"

Aircraft Type:	Bf 109 E-3
Purpose:	Single seater fighter
Crew:	One
Engine plant:	1 x DB 601A or Aa (699-864 kW, 950-1175 hp)
Wingspan:	9.9 m
Length:	8.8 m
Height:	2.5 m
Wing area:	16.4 sq.m
Top speed:	555 kms/hr at 5000 m altitude
Cruising speed:	400 kms/hr (low level)
Landing speed:	111 kms/hr
Rate of climb to 5000 m:	5.7 mins
Weight empty:	2050 kgs
All-up weight:	2608 kgs
Service ceiling:	10,500 m
Range:	600 kms (max)
Armament:	2 x MG 17 (fuselage), 2 x MG FF (wings)

The development of the Bf 109 E began with the trial of a DB 601A engine in the air frames of two B-0 (V-15 and V-15a). These were machines of the E-0 nil series of ten (up to V-22). The prototype (D-IPKY) was a converted B-1. The first series version had fixed armament of four MG 17's. As from E-3 the two MGs in the wings were replaced by two MG FF's. The more efficient DB 601N motor was installed as from the E-4. The E-1/B, E-3/B and E-4 B versions flew as fighter-bombers. E-5 was a short-range reconnaissance aircraft with a film camera (Rb) 21/28, the E-6 having a DB 601N motor and mechanised camera. E-7 and E-8 were "fighters with enhanced range" for which they carried a disposable 300-litre supplementary fuel tank hung below the fuselage. The long-range

The Bf 109 E-1 and E-3 was the standard fighter of the Luftwaffe during operations over Western Europe.

reconnaissance version E-9 was fitted with a 50 x 50 (Rb) film camera. Production of the Bf 109 E was handled at Arado, Erla, Fieseler and Messerschmitt as well as at the aircraft works at Wiener Neustadt. The Bf 109 E series was the standard fighter of the German Luftwaffe from 1939 to 1941 when replaced by the Bf 109 F. A number of Bf 109 E's were passed to Axis or neutral countries, most of them to Bulgaria, Rumania and Switzerland.

Above: The size of the Bf 109 E made maintenance in the field easy.

Left: The fighting value of the Bf 109 E was increased markedly by the installation of two MG FF's in the wings.

Bf 109 T-1 and T-2

The Bf 109 C-1/V-17 (Works Nr 1776, D-IYMS) was fitted experimentally in 1937 with catapult fittings and arresting hook for use aboard aircraft carriers. Another six experimental machines (B/E series) followed. The longer wings provided substantially improved flying characteristics to the Bf 109 E. The E-3/N seemed an especially good starting point for the series conversion. Only seven of 70 Bf 109 T-1's ordered as carrier aircraft had folding wings. The other 63 flew as single-seater fighters of the T-2 model. The aircraft were collected between February and June 1941 and went mainly to 11./JG 11 and 1./JG 77 operating from Norway. The available T-2 machines were surprisingly removed from operations at the end of 1942 and converted into Bf 109 T-1's at Fieseler's. After the carrier project was abandoned, they were rebuilt as T-2's or passed to training schools.

Aircraft Type:	Bf 109 T-2
Purpose:	Single seater fighter
Crew:	One
Engine plant:	1 x DB 601N (699-938 kW, 950-1275 hp)
Wingspan:	11.08 m
Length:	8.76 m
Height:	2.6 m
Wing area:	17.3 sq.m
Top speed:	498 kms/hr at 5,000 m altitude
Cruising speed:	405 kms/hr (low level)
Landing speed:	111kms/hr
Rate of climb to 5,000 m:	5.5 mins
Weight empty:	2250 kgs
All-up weight:	3800 kgs
Service ceiling:	10,500 m
Range:	700 kms
Armament:	2 x MG 17 (fuselage), 2 x MG FF (wings)

The Bf 109 T-1 was originally intended to operate from an aircraft carrier.

Bf 109 with radial motor

As the result of an instruction by Generalluftzeugmeister Ernst Udet, the Bf 109 V-21 (Works Nr 1770, D-IFKQ) was fitted experimentally with a BMW 139 or BMW 801 radial motor to examine its flight characteristics. Because the BMW 801 was far from ready in the autumn of 1938, the RLM proposed instead a Pratt & Whitney Twin Wasp SC-G. The experimental aircraft was completed in 1939 and flown on 18 August that year by Dr Wurster and Fritz Wendel. The prototype then went first to the experimental centre at Rechlin and afterwards the DVL at Berlin-Adlershof. Later the machine (KB+II) was passed on to Braunschweig-Völkenrode to be used by manufacturers for experience of the radial engine. The only true Bf 109 X with BMW 801 A-0 was flown by Fritz Wendel from 2 September 1940. This was the converted

Aircraft Type:	Bf 109 X
Purpose:	Experimental aircraft with radial motor
Crew:	One
Engine plant:	1 x BMW 801 A-0 (919-993 kW, 1250-1350 hp)
Wingspan:	9.33 m
Length:	Unknown
Height:	2.5 m
Wing area:	16.3 sq.m
Top speed:	525 kms/hr at 4,000m altitude
Cruising speed:	400 kms/hr (low level)
Landing speed:	110 kms/hr
Rate of climb to 5,000 m:	Unknown
Weight empty:	2050 ks
All-up weight:	2600 kgs
Service ceiling and Range:	Unknown
Armament:	None

Bf 109 E (Works Nr 5608, D-ITXP). With the introduction of the Fw 190 A-1, the series production of the Bf 109 with radial motor was abandoned.

The installation of radial motors on the Bf 109 was only experimental.

Bf 109 F-0 to F-6 "Friedrich"

Aircraft Type:	Bf 109 F-2
Purpose:	Single seater fighter
Crew:	One
Engine plant:	1 x DB 601N (865 kW, 1175 hp)
Wingspan:	9.92 m
Length:	8.94 m
Height:	2.5 m
Wing area:	16.02 sq.m
Top speed:	590 kms/hr at 5,000 m
Altitude:	495 kms/hr (low level)
Landing speed:	110 kms/hr
Rate of climb to 5,000 m:	4.8 mins
Weight empty:	2480 kgs
All-up weight:	3200 kgs
Service ceiling:	11,000 m
Range:	1050 kms
Armament:	1 x MG 151 (fuselage), 2 x MG 17 (fuselage)

The finest Bf 109 in terms of streamlining must be the Friedrich. Following the experience of the previous year of the war, from December 1940 work began on the Bf 109 F. This version had new wings with rounded end caps, a new motor and propellor hub and a redesigned spinner. The fuel capacity was increasd to 400 litres, an improved radio installed (FuG VIIa and Patin-compass unit) and an MG FF mechanised cannon. After a nil series (F-0) of ten machines, series production of the F-1 began at the end of 1941, this being a fighter with a DB 601N inverted-V motor. In the subsequent F-2 version the MG FF was replaced by an MG 151. The machines of the F-3 and all further series had the DB 601E engine plant. The Bf 109 F-4 had a

This early Bf 109 F prototype shows the aerodynamic elegance of the fighter.

gondola for an MG 151/20 or film cameras. A conversion, the F-4/U1 had two MG 131's in place of the MG 17's. The final two versions served as fast short-range reconnaissance aircraft. Thus the Bf 109 F-5 armed with only two MG 17's, and the F-6 corresponding to the F-4 were provided with hand or film cameras. For example these machines were used operationally at 1.(F)/122. As a fighter, the Bf 109 served in all theatres of war. The Luftwaffe received about 2,400 of them.

Above: During winter operations the undercarriage covering was removed temporarily.

Left: This Bf 109 F of JG 3 "Udet" has five claimed kills painted on the rudder.

Bf 109 G-0 to G-14 "Gustav"

The most prolific series was the Bf 109 G to combat the increased efficiency of Allied fighter aircraft. The new version was distinguished by the more powerful DB 605A engine. Every attempt was made to match the newest Allied piston aircraft by constant increase in performance: a larger supercharger, the use of C-3 fuel and MW 50 supplementary injection. The GM-1 process (injection of nitrous oxide) was also employed. The Bf 109 G-1, G-3 and G-5 versions were fitted with a pressure cabin and could be armed with up to three MG 151 and two MG 17's. The G-2 and G-4 of similar construction lacked the GM-1 installation and pressure cabin. With effect from the Bf 109 G-5 the two MG 17 on the upper fuselage were

Aircraft Type:	Bf 109 G-6
Purpose:	One-seater fighter
Crew:	One
Engine plant:	1 x DB 605A (1103 kW, 1500 hp)
Wingspan:	9.92 m
Length:	9.02 m
Height:	3.2 m
Wing area:	16.05 sq.m
Top speed:	630 kms/hr at 8,000 m altitude, 506 kms/hr (low level)
Landing speed:	110 kms/hr
Rate of climb to 6,000 m:	6 mins
Weight empty:	2275 kgs
All-up weight:	3200 kgs
Service ceiling:	11,300 m
Range:	560 kms at 6,000 m
Armament:	1 x MG 151/20 (mechanised gun), 2 x MG 131 (fuselage weapons)

This overhauled Bf 109 G-6 was flown by the Swiss.

Bf 109 G's no longer battle-worthy were converted into two-seater training machines (Bf 109 G-12).

The use of the Erla-cowling improved the pilot's vision significantly.

replaced by the more powerful MG 131. Because of their bulk the belt feeds were housed in two blisters. The additional equipment and the reinforcement to the wings led to constant increases in the maximum take-off weight up to 4000 kgs with the G-6. The Bf 109 G-6 was amongst the most ubiquitous fighters in the Luftwaffe squadrons everywhere. As with most Bf 109 G's the machine could be fitted with a sand filter for tropical operations.

Apart from an ETC 500/IXb for a disposable container or bombload up to 500 kgs, gondola-weapons such as the MG 151/20 MG could always be fitted. Some of the machines later had a DB 605 AS engine and large rudder unit. In the fast reconnaissance role the Bf 109 G-8 flew with two film cameras. Bf 109 G-10 was a further development of the G-6 as a light fighter. The machine was made up of parts of the G-2, G-6, G-14 and K-4.

This Bf 109 G-6 of 1 Grp/JG1 finished a flight on its nose.

Bf 109 H-0 to H-5

The "Special High Altitude Fighter" was a progression from the "G" model with much larger wings. Consideration had also been given to a much more efficient high-altitude engine, eventually the DB 628 with a two-stage supercharger. In the summer of 1943 Bf 109 G-3 (V-49) was used as the mock-up, and G-3 (V-50) (DN+KD) flew on 12 May 1943 with a DB 628 experimental engine. In July 1943 work was suspended due to engine problems, and the next machine, Bf 109 G5 (PV+JB) became the first H-0 of the nil series. Trials with it began in November 1943 and terminated with a collapse of the undercarriage in July 1944. Previously a successor, Bf 109 (V-55) had been destroyed by a bomb on 25 February 1944, and the third survived little longer, and crashed on 14 April 1944. The completely revised Bf 109 HV-1 (Works Nr 16281, SP+EB) was destroyed in an air raid on 14 August 1944. The project

was passed to Blohm & Voss where the development proceeded under the designation BV 155. The planned versions H-1 to H-5 went no further than the drawing board.

Aircraft Type:	BF 109 V-54
Purpose:	Experimental high altitude fighter
Crew:	One
Engine plant:	1 x DB 628 experimental engine (1085 kW, 1476 hp)
Wingspan:	21 m
Length:	10.25 m
Height:	4.1 m
Wing area:	39.3 sq.m
Top speed:	560 kms/hr at 8000 m, 423 kms/hr (low level)
Landing speed:	110 kms/hr
Rate of climb to 12,000 m:	25.4 mins
Weight empty:	3682 kgs
All-up weight:	4250 kgs
Service ceiling:	14,800 m
Range:	512 kms at 6000 m
Armament:	1 x MG 151/20 and 2 x MG 131

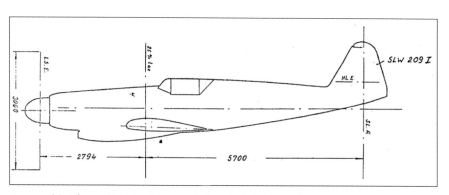

Drawing of the Bf 109 H high altitude fighter which received a DB 629 V19 engine.

Bf 109 K-0 to K-14 "Karl"

The last Bf 109 version to appear in any numbers was a Bf 109 G-10 and G-14 hybrid. For the nil series, ten G-10 were fitted with a DB 605D engine. The versions with a pressurised cabin (K-1, K-3, K-5 etc) were abandoned early on. The more elaborately equipped K-2 had either a DB 605 DM, DB or DC engine and MW 50 additional injection. It is thought that only a few of these were built, the later principal version being the well-armed K-4. Fitments here were options for an ETC 500/IX for bombloads (R1), a disposable container (R2) and an armaments gondola for two cannons (R3). Two series aircraft of the K-6 version were to have been ready by the end of April 1945, but construction work on the K-8 to K-14 was discontinued. By April 1945 about 700 K-4 had been built.

Aircraft Type:	Bf 109 K-4
Purpose:	Light fighter
Crew:	One
Engine plant:	1 x DB 605D (1324 kW, 1800 hp)
Wingspan:	9.02 m
Length:	9 m
Height:	2.35 m
Wing area:	16.02 sq.m
Top speed:	680 kms/hr
Cruising speed:	525 kms/hr
Landing speed:	120 kms/hr
Rate of climb to 6000 m:	5.8 mins
Weight empty:	2755 kgs
All-up weight:	3400 kgs
Servce ceiling:	11,250 m
Range:	900 kms
Armament:	1 x Mk 108 (mechanised cannon) 2 x MG 131, fuselage

The development section devised an experimetnal aerodynamic engine cowling for the DB 605.

The K-4 version was the most powerful version of the Bf 109.

Bf 110 Experimental Aircraft

The RLM required "heavy fighters" to go with the light single-seaters, and despite the competition the contract for the future Bf 110 was awarded to Messerschmitt in the summer of 1934. Bf 110 V-1 (Works Nr 868, D-AHOA) with two Jumo 210 engines was flown on 12 May 1936 by Dr Hermann Wurster. From October 1937 the machine underwent weapons trials at the Tarnewitz experimental centre. Bf 110 V-2 was used principally for the testing of equipment. The first of two Bf 110 fighters with two DB 601 engines, the V-3, to be fitted later with two DB 600, served as a fore-runner to the C series. V6 and V8 were the first experimental units for this version. Bf 110 V-4 fitted with two Jumo 210G engines was the fore-runner for the B series. The Bf 110 SV-9 "heavy dive-bomber" attracted no interest at the Reich Air Ministry.

Aircraft Type:	Bf 110 V-1
Purpose:	Fighter-bomber "Destroyer" (experimental)
Crew:	Two
Engine plant:	2 x Jumo 10 (each 363-470 kW, 480-640 hp)
Wingspan:	16.9 m
Length:	12 m
Height:	3.3 m
Wing area:	Unknown
Top speed:	465 kms/hr at 4,000 metres altitude
Cruising speed:	435 kms/hr
Landing speed:	120 kms/hr
Rate of climb to 4,000 m:	Unknown
Weight empty:	3,800 kgs
All-up weight:	5,400 kgs
Service ceiling:	7,000 m
Range:	About 1000 kms no armament

On 1 October 1937 nine experimental machines were ordered. Numerous prototypes were to follow which formed the basis of the various series production.

The experimental Bf 110 V-3 was fitted with two DB 600.

Bf 110 A-0 to B-3

Between July 1937 and March 1938 only six machines (Work Nrs 910 to 915) were built at Messerschmitt Augsburg from the nil series Bf 110 A-0. Two Jumo 210 engines were fitted since the hoped for DB 601's were not available. On account of this problem, the machines fell well below the expectations of the RLM. Bf 110 V-7 was the prototype for the B series: Works Nrs. 918 and 941 with Jumo 210G engines were the experimental versions. Relatively few versions of the B series came off the assembly line, at Messerschmitt Augsburg about 24 B-0 and B-1 (Works Nrs 917 to 942). Production was then undertaken by the Gothaer Waggonfabrik which between April and September 1939 turned out another 62 machines (Works Nrs 1731 to 1792). Once the production of the DB 601 engine was possible in large numbers, the Bf 110 C-1 replaced the B-1. Available B-1's were converted into reconnaissance machines (B-2) and trainers (B-3).

Aircraft Type:	Bf 110 B-1
Purpose:	Destroyer (fighterbomber) series production
Crew:	Two
Engine plant:	2 x Jumo 210G (each 508-537 kW, 690-730 hp)
Wingspan:	16.9 m
Length:	12.07 m
Height:	3.3 m
Wing area:	38.4 m
Top speed:	480 kms/hr at 4,000 m altitude
Cruising speed:	432 kms/hr
Landing speed:	140 kms/hr
Rate of climb to 3,000 m:	3.5 mins
Weight empty:	4150 kgs
All-up weight:	5650 kgs
Service ceiling:	8,000+ m
Range:	1,200+ kms
Armament:	2 x MG FF and 4 x MG 17 (fixed), 1 x MG 15, (manoeuvrable)

The Bf 110 B-1 (D-AAPY) was tested using an Mk 101 cannon.

Bf 110 C-1 to C-7

The first two-seater Bf 110 C's produced in large numbers as heavy fighters (also known as "Destroyers") had a fixed armament of four MG 17 and two MG FF. A manoeuvrable MG 15 mounted to face astern was operated by the radio operator/air-gunner. The Bf 110 C-1 was fitted with two DB 601 B-1 engines. From the beginning of 1939 a total of 195 of these aircraft were built at Focke-Wulf, Messerschmitt, Gotha and MIAG. These were followed by 339 Bf 110 C-2's and 149 C-4's, which were "Destroyers" with improved MG FF"M" armament, and 100 C-5 reconnaissance aircraft with an inboard camera unit. Production began in June 1940. In the summer of 1940 only 16 of the C-6 low-level attack aircraft with an MK 101 under the fuselage were built. Series production of the C-7, a fighter-bomber, began in July 1940 and manufacture of the Bf 110 C came to an end in January 1941. The C-7 could carry two SC-500 bombs and was equipped from existing Bf 110 C-4/b aircraft.

Aircraft Type:	Bf 110 C-1
Purpose:	Destroyer (heavy fighter)
Crew:	Two
Engine plant:	2 x DB 601A (each 699-864 kW: 950-1175 hp)
Wingspan:	16.28 m
Length:	12.07 m
Height:	3.3 m
Wing area:	38.4 sq.m
Top speed:	545 kms/hr at 4,000 m altitude
Cruising speed:	445 kms/hr
Landing speed:	120 kms/hr
Rate of climb to 4,000 m:	3.5 mins
Weight empty:	4600 kgs
All-up weight:	6050 kgs
Service ceiling:	8,500+ m
Range:	850 kms
Armament:	2 x MG FF and 4 x MG 17 (fixed) 1 x MG 15 (manoeuvrable)

A Bf 110 C, here an aircraft of II./ZG 76, during the campaign in the West.

Removing the engine of a Bf 110 C using a tripod and pulley.

Bf 110 D-0 to D-4

As operational areas expanded, the range of the Bf 110 C became inadequate. For this reason the Bf 110 D-0 was given a 1200-litre supplementary fuel tank fitted below the fuselage known as the "Dackelbauch" (the dachshund's stomach). Drive was two DB 601 inverted-V engines. As from the D-2 the fuselage tank was replaced by two 900-litre disposable tanks located under each wing. Production of the Bf 110 D-version began at Messerschmitt Augsburg with an enormous nil-series of 83 machines in March 1940. This was due to the urgent demand for destroyer aircraft and long-range night fighters. After this came 21 D-1 delivered by Focke-Wulf in the spring of 1940. After 73 D-2 destroyers and night fighters, and around 260 D-3 fighter-bombers, had been turned out the production concluded in March 1941. If required, the machines could be fitted with a release system for up to two 500 kg bombs. The 900-litre additional tanks were now replaced by two lighter 300-litre disposable tanks. The D-3 was longer in the fuselage, which had hold space for a rubber dinghy. Only six aircraft of the D-4 series were produced at Messerschmitt.

Aircraft Type:	Bf 110 D-0
Purpose:	Long-range destroyer and fighter-bomber
Crew:	Two
Engine plant:	2 x DB 601A (each 669-864 kW, 950-1175 hp)
Wingspan:	16.28 m
Length:	12.07 m
Height:	3.3 m
Wing area:	38.4 sq.m
Top speed:	540 kms/hr at 4,000 metres altitude
Cruising speed:	440 kms/hr
Landing speed:	120 kms/hr
Rate of climb to 4,000 m:	3.8 mins
Weight empty:	4800 kgs
All-up weight:	6450 kgs
Service ceiling:	8500 m
Range:	1600+ kms
Armament:	2 x MG FF and 4 x MG 17 (fixed) and 1 x MG 15 (manoeuvrable)

The need for a greater range was met by the Bf 110 D.

Bf 110 E-1 to E-3

The E-version was based on the C-version but with a strengthened airframe to take a heavier bombload than previously. Apart from two 500 kg bombs under the fuselage, four 50-kg bombs could be carried under the outer section of the wings increasing the bomb payload to 1200 kgs. The armament was unchanged From August 1940 over 380 aircraft of the E-1 series were produced at Messerschmitt. This was now a utility aircraft used operationally as a destroyer, fighter-bomber, long-range reconnaissance machine and night fighter. The next series (E-2) was produced at Gotha, Focke-Wulf, MIAG and Messerschmitt from February 1941. The third and last version, Bf 110 E-3, a long-range reconnaissance aircraft with reduced armament, of which 190 units were manufactured, completed the E-production in October 1941.

Aircraft Type:	Bf 110 E-1
Purpose:	Bomber and reconnaissance aircraft
Crew:	Two
Engine plant:	2 x DB 601A (each 669-864 kW, 950-1175 hp)
Wingspan:	16.28 m
Length:	12.07 m
Height:	3.3 m
Wing area:	38.4 sq.m
Top speed:	540 kms/hr at 4000 m altitude
Cruising speed:	440 kms/hr
Landing speed:	120 kms/hr
Rate of climb to 4,000 m:	3.9 mins
Weight empty:	4800+ kgs
All-up weight:	7500+ kgs
Service ceiling:	9000+ m
Range:	1000+ km
Armament:	2 x MG FF and 4 x MG 17 (fixed), 1 x MG 15 (manouevrable)

The Bf 110 E-3 was also used as a fast reconnaissance aircraft in North Africa.

Bf 110 F-2 to F-4

Series production of the initially two-seater Bf 110 F was in essence a Bf 110 E of increased fighting value with increased armour and two series-produced disposable fuel tanks at the outer ends of the wings. As a rule the machine was equipped with two DB 601 F engines. After the F-1, a fighter-bomber, was dropped, from March 1942 work proceeded on 190 Bf 110 F-2 at Gotha. This was a destroyer and night fighter intended to intercept heavy four-engined bombers. The Luther-Works at Braunschweig made the F-3 from June 1942. This machine could be used in the reconnaissance role with great range and had a film camera unit in the fuselage. The next and last version of the F-series, the Bf 110 F-4, flew as a night-fighter with a three-man crew. Gotha produced 279 of the F-4 until December 1942: these were used in the night fighter squadrons of the Luftwaffe.

Aircraft Type:	Bf 110 F-2
Purpose:	Destroyer
Crew:	Two
Engine plant:	2 x DB 601F (each 993 kW, 2 x 1350 hp)
Wingspan:	16.28 m
Length:	12.07 m
Height:	3.3 m
Wing area:	38.4 sq.m
Top speed:	570 kms/hr at 5000 m altitude
Cruising speed:	520 kms/hr at 4000 m altitude
Landing speed:	120 kms/hr
Rate of climb to 6,000 m:	9 mins
Weight empty:	6700 kgs
All-up weight:	9000+ kgs
Service ceiling:	10,000 m
Range:	1000+ kms
Armament:	2 x MG FF and 4 x MG 17 (fixed), 2 x MG 151/20 in a tub below the fuselage, 1 x MG 15 (manoeuvrable)

This Bf 110 F of ZG26 "Horst Wessel" flew protection over the Mediterranean for Ju 52/3m transports.

Bf 110 G-0 to G-4

The last series of the Bf 110 appeared in the summer of 1942. The machine was based on the Bf 110 F with a more powerful engine plant of two DB 605B-1. The obsolete MG FF "M" guns were replaced by MG 151/20 cannons, and mostly from the beginning an MG 81 Z, superior to the former MG 15, was fitted into the rear-gunner's position. The nil-series, used to see how the new engine plant handled, was limited to only six aircraft, these being built at Gotha from June 1942. The series G-2 followed, shared between Luther and Gotha which produced 797 machines from December 1942. These were reconnaissance aircraft which could fit equally well into the fast bomber role with up to a one-tonne payload. Only 172 G-3 long range reconnaissance machines followed, from

As "bomber-formation destroyers" machines such as this Bf 110 G-2 were fitted with up to four rocket launchers.

Aircraft Type:	Bf 110 G-4
Purpose:	Night-fighter
Crew:	Two
Engine plant:	2 x DB 605 B-1 (each 1085 kW, 1475 hp)
Wingspan:	16.28 m
Length:	12.07 m
Height:	3.30m
Wing area:	38.4 sq.m
Top speed:	595 kms/hr at 6,000 m altitude
Cruising speed:	440 kms/hr
Landing speed:	120 kms/hr
Rate of climb to 4000 m altitude:	3.9 mins
Weight empty:	5600 kgs
All-up weight:	7800 kgs
Service ceiling:	11,500 m
Range:	900+ kms
Armament:	2 x MG 151/20 (fixed), 2 x MG 151/20 (additional) and 1 x MG 81Z (manoeuvrable), weaponry able to fire upwards at an oblique angle optional

January 1943 at Gotha. The last series run was the Bf 110 G-4, produced by Gotha and Luther between January 1943 and April 1945. About 2,300 of these machines, the greatest total of any Bf 110 series, were completed. They were flown mainly as night fighters. Some were fitted with the upwards-slanted armament, either two MG FF or two bigger MK 108, others had two additional MG 151/120 guns installed under the fuselage. Together with the Ju 88 G-6 from 1944, this machine was one of the standard night fighters of the German Luftwaffe. Planning was under way for an improved version of the G-4 and at least one prototype was finished.

Only a few Bf 110 G aircraft were fitted with two MG 151/20 in the nose and a 3.7 cannon.

As the war went on, the radar aerials, such as that fitted to this Bf 110 G-4, became ever more comprehensive.

Bf 161

Messerschmitt received the specifications for a high-altitude long-range reconnaissance aircraft, the future Bf 161, in August 1935. The RLM was counting on a full-size mock-up of the P 1035 three months later. Messerschmitt was also asked to manufacture a prototype with two Jumo 210, the Bf 161 V-1, and another with two DB 600, the Bf 161 V-2. In October 1937 the RLM decided not to proceed with the Bf 161 for the Luftwaffe in favour of the Do 17P. Nevertheless work on the Bf 161 went ahead. The maiden flight of the three-seater Bf 161 V-1 (Works Nr 811, D-AABA) on 9 March 1938 was made by Dr Hermann Wurster. In November 1939 the unarmed machine was passed to the assessment centre at Rechlin. Bf 161 V-2 (Works Nr 812, D-AOFI) was first flown on 30 August 1938. The preference of the RLM for the Do 17P long-range reconnaissance machine signalled the end for the Bf 161, and during the development of the Me 163 it was used as a tug.

Aircraft Type:	Bf 161 V-2
Purpose:	Long range reconnaissance (experimental)
Crew:	Three
Engine plant:	2 x DB 600A (each 570-35 kW, 775-1000 hp)
Wingspan:	17.16 m
Length:	12.82 m
Height:	3.3 m
Wing area:	38.4 sq.m
Top speed:	490 kms/hr at 4000 m altitude
Cruising speed:	350 kms/hr
Landing speed:	110 kms/hr
Rate of climb to 3000 m:	5 mins
Weight empty:	3250 kgs
All-up weight:	4890 kgs
Service ceiling:	8000 m
Range:	Unknown
Armament:	Preparations to install a manoeuevrable MG 15

The development of the Bf 161 was broken off prematurely.

Bf 162

Design work on the Bf 162, which like the Bf 161 was developed from the Bf 110, began in the summer of 1935. This was a twin-engined fast bomber intended to compete against the Ju 88. In 1936 the RLM gave Messerschmitt an order for five experimental aircraft and a series run of 65 of which the first, Bf 162 V-1 (Works Nr 817, DAIXA) was flown by Dr Wurster on 26 February 1937. Propulsion was two DB 600 inverted-V engines. The Bf 162 V-2 (Works Nr 818, D-AOBE) followed towards the end of October 1937. This machine was later used for towing the Me 163 during its development. The V-3 (Works Nr 819, D-AOVI) was finished and underwent trials from July 1938. On 9 March 1938 the RLM notified the cancellation of the contract in favour of the Ju 88 as its fast bomber. Although the performance was to some extent better than the Junkers machine, the total commitment of the Messerschmitt

Aircraft Type:	Bf 162 V-1
Purpose:	Fast bomber (experimental)
Crew:	Three
Engine plant:	2 x B 600A (each 570-35 kW, 775-1000 hp)
Wingspan:	17.12 m
Length:	12.45 m
Height:	3.3 m
Wing area:	38.4 sq.m
Top speed:	495 kms/hr at 4000 m altitude
Cruising speed:	360 kms/hr
Landing speed:	110 kms/hr
Rate of climb to 3000 m:	5 mins
Weight empty:	3250 kgs
All-up weight:	6490 kgs
Service ceiling:	8000 m
Range:	Unknown
Armament:	2 x MG 15

Works to producing the Bf 109 militated against further development of the Bf 162. Rechlin received the third and last machine in 1939.

There was no need for the fast bomber (here is Bf 162 V-2) since better types were available.

Bf 163

In September 1935, the Messerschmitt Works received a contract to build three prototypes of a three-seater communications aircraft (P 1051). The machine was to be suitable to fly short-range reconnaissance. The extremely short take-off and slow-speed flight characteristics of the planned machine required considerable expenditure and effort. Even the Aerodynamic Experimental Institute at Göttingen and the Lilienthal Gesellschaft were co-opted into the work on the Bf 163. Because of the total commitment to another project, Messerschmitt passed the development to the firm of Rohrbach Metallflugzeugbau GmbH, Berlin. The Bf 163 V-1 was subsequently built at the Weser Flugzeugbau GmbH, Lemwerder, and first flown on 19 February 1938 by Gerhard Hubrich. The flight characteristics of the Bf 163 were not found satisfactory, and later flights piloted by Dr Wurster also failed to convince. Some components of the V-2 and V-3 were

Aircraft Type:	Bf 163 V-1
Purpose:	Communications aircraft and short range reconnaissance
Crew:	Two to three
Engine plant:	1 x Argus As 10C (177 kW 240 hp)
Wingspan:	13.58 m
Length:	9.75 m
Height:	Unknown
Wing area:	22.8 sq.m
Top speed:	200 kms/hr
Cruising speed:	170 kms/hr
Landing speed:	50 kms/hr
Rate of climb to 3000 m:	Unknown
Weight empty:	900 kgs
All-up weight:	1310 kgs
Service ceiling:	Unknown
Range:	450 kms
Armament:	None

manufactured but did not reach the assembly stage. On 29 September 1939 the Bf 163 V-1 (D-IUCY) was passed to the aviation technical school at Munich and nearly all the files and plans destroyed.

Development of the Bf 163, a light communications aircraft, was quickly given up.

Me 163 A-0

The Me 163 was an idea originating from Dr-Ing. Alexander Lippisch in the early 1920s. After machines such as the Storch I to X and the Delta-series, the DFS 194 appeared for consideration at the Deutsche Forschungsanstalt für Segelflug (German Research Institute for Gliding). From 2 January 1939 intensive work was begun at Messerschmitt on a rocket-propelled tail-less fighter. From this "Project X" emerged the Me 163. For reasons of security the first prototype was designated V-4. This was one of ten machines (A-0) of the nil-series. Testing of the Me 163 AV-4 (Works Nr 1630000001 KE+SW) began on 13 February 1941. On 2 October 1941 it broke the world speed record with a flight at 1003 kms/hr. The prototypes were used primarily for testing purposes but also for the training of pilots. One of the nil-series was fitted in March 1945 with two R4M

Aircraft Type:	Me 163 AV (A-0)
Purpose:	Localized shortrange fighter
Crew:	One
Engine plant:	1 x HWK R II-203 (7.35 kN, 750 hp)
Wingspan:	9.25 m
Length:	5.25 m
Height:	2.2 m
Wing area:	17.51 sq.m
Top speed:	850 kms/hr
Cruising speed:	(!)
Landing speed:	170 kms/hr
Rate of climb to 3850 m:	1 min
Weight empty:	1140 kgs
All-up weight:	2200 kgs
Service ceiling:	in excess of 6000 m
Range:	less than 75 kms
Armament:	2 x MG 151 and 2 x RZ 65 batteries (planned)

racks below the wings for preliminary tests of the new armament, the others remained unarmed. The installation of two MG 151/20 and RZ 65 batteries was planned, but shelved on account of the Me 163B.

The first Me 163 AV-4 flow on 13 February 1941.

Me 163 B-0 to B-2

The German Luftwaffe employed the Me 163 B as a "Homeland Protector" for the immediate air defence of important industrial targets. The construction of the Me 163 B-0 began in early December 1941. Most of the early nil-series were used as experimental aircraft to test out the rocket-motor and for a tactical assessment of the Me 163 as an operational machine at Erprobungskommando 16. The Me 163 had a detachable wheeled chassis for take-off and a well-sprung skid for landings on a grass strip. The first three, Me 163 B-0 to B-2, were tail-less machines with a dual-substance rocket drive conceived by HWK of Kiel. The first aircraft of

Aircraft Type:	Me 163 B-1
Purpose:	"Homeland protector" (Fighter to protect local industrial installations)
Crew:	One
Propulsion:	1 x HK 109-509 A-1 (16.7 k 1700 hp)
Wingspan:	9.32 m
Length:	5.92 m
Height:	2.8 m
Wing area:	19.6 sq.m
Top speeds:	830 kms/hr (low level), 960 kms/hr at 3000 m altitude
Landing speed:	160 kms/hr
Rate of climb to 12,000 m:	3.5 mins
Weight empty:	1910 kgs
All-up weight:	4310 kgs
Service ceiling:	2,000 m
Range:	75-100 kms
Armament:	2 x MK 108 or 2 x MG 151/.

The Me 163 B, here a machine attached to JG 400 during lengthy ground manouevres.

the series were gliders towed up to altitude for testing. This began on 26 June 1942. As a result of problems with the rocket motor, series production was held back for almost two years. On 31 April 1944 1.Staffel/JG 400 received their first thirteen Me 163. By 8 September 1944 pilots had three confirmed victories. Operations ebbed increasingly from the beginning of 1945 due to fuel shortages. A total of about 470 Me 163 were built.

Side profile of the Me 163 B, today at a museum.

With two torpedo-bombs BT 700 and BT 1400 it was even planned to use the Me 163 against shipping along the coasts.

Me 163 C-0 and D-0

In daily use several weaknesses were noted of the Me 163 B. In particular the fuel for the HWK 509 A-1 had proved extremely dangerous. The relatively small amount of fuel allowed only relatively brief missions, so that the range of the machine was rarely more than 80 kms. In January 1942 work began on a version with greater fuel capacity and an additional motor for slower speeds, but not until 25 May 1944 was the Me 163 C-0, developed from the Me 163 B V1-a, tested in towed flight. Subsequently another two C-machines were built. The disadvantage of having no retractable undercarriage was overcome with the D-series. The first machine, which had the look of the planned Me 163 D-0 about it, was first flown on 3 November 1944. Two prototypes, the former BV 13 and 18, were converted. Because of the planned imminent introduction of the more efficient Ju 248 (Me 263), neither the Me 163 C nor the Me 163 D came near series production.

Aircraft Type:	Me 163 C-0 (Conversion fro. Me 163 BV1-a)
Purpose:	Fighter to protect local installations
Crew:	One
Propulsion:	1 x HWK 109-509C (19.5 kN 2000 hp)
Wingspan:	9.8 m
Length:	7.02 m
Height:	2.9 m
Wing area:	20.05 sq.m
Top speeds:	800 kms/hr (low level), 960 kms/hr at 6000 m altitude
Landing speed:	160 kms/hr
Rate of climb to 12,000 m:	About 3.5 mins
Weight empty:	1950 kgs
All-up weight:	5000 kgs
Service ceiling:	15,000 m
Range:	175 kms
Armament:	Up to four Mk 108 planned

Only prototypes of the Me 163 C and D were manufactured.

Me 163 S

When the Me 163 B was introduced the need arose for a two-seater version to train pilots for operations. In the spring of 1944 sketches were produced for a series of converted existing Me 163 aircraft. Behind the former cabin a second, slightly raised seat was installed below a plexiglass hood. The first of 42 planned Me 163 S was completed in August 1944 at Staaken near Berlin and flown there on numerous occasions until the beginning of April 1945. In the spring of 1945 two more Me 163 S were located one each at II and III Groups, Ergänzungsjagdgeschwader (EJG) 2; and at the beginning of 1945 another two went to the Peenemünde-West assessment centre for test purposes. Apparently only seven series aircraft were manufactured, the Me 163 losing favour once the Me 262 A-1a was operational. At least one intact Me 163 S was captured by the Red Army and often flew in the Soviet Union from the summer of 1945.

Aircraft Type:	Me 163 S
Purpose:	Trainer
Crew:	Two
Propulsion:	None
Wingspan:	9.3 m
Length:	5.92 m
Height:	2.5 m
Wing area:	19.6 sq.m
Landing speed:	160 kms/hr
Details of weight:	ceiling etc unknown
Range:	about 50 kms

Less than ten units of the Me 163 S two-seater trainer were made available.

Me 208 and Nord 1101

Aircraft Type:	Me 208 V-1
Purpose:	Communications aircraft
Crew:	One
Engine plant:	1 x Argus As 10C (176 kW, 240 hp)
Wingspan:	11.5 m
Length:	8.85 m
Height:	3.35 m
Wing area:	17.4 sq.m
Top speed:	305 kms/hr
Cruising speed:	275 kms/hr
Landing speed:	110 kms/hr
Rate of climb to 3,000 m:	14 mins
Weight empty:	945 kgs
All-up weight:	1585 kgs
Service ceiling:	5900 m
Range:	1300 kms

The Me 208 represented the attempt to replicate the Me 108 with a nose wheel and extended range of around 1,300 kms by the installation of larger fuel tanks. Messerschmitt had the project until 1941 when the practical work was hived out to France. The engine plant was to have been either an Argus As 10C or a Hirth HM 508. First at SNCAN at Les Mureaux, a Bf 108 D-1 was prepared for testing with a nose wheel. The initial flight in October 1942 proved successful with no negative consequences resulting from the conversion. Building on the earlier results SNCAN now went ahead with the Me 208 V-1 fitted with an Argus As 10C engine. The prototype made a maiden flight in July 1943. Work was suspended the same year once

An aircraft considered modern for those times, the Me 208 fell victim to the war situation.

operational machines, and particularly fighters, enjoyed absolute priority. After the German Wehrmacht withdrew from France, work began again on the machine, now known as Nord 1101 fitted with a SNECMA-Renault 6 Q-Motor (176 kW, 240 hp). 200 of these aircraft "Nordalpha" and "Ramier" were ordered and built for the French forces. Individual machines were flown from 1959 as test carriers for a Turboméca propellor-turbine of the "Astazou" type. Together with the continued line of Bf 108 D-1 renamed Nord 1000, better variants with more powerful engines were produced such as the "Pinguin I" and "II".

The development of the Me 208 was continued by the French and flown for many years by them under the designation Nord 1101.

Me 209

After the record flight of the Bf 109 V-13, from 1937 Willy Messerschmitt formed the intention to keep the world speed record for himself. The first flight of the Me 209 V-1 (Works Nr. 1185 D-INJR) was piloted by Dr Hermann Wurster on 1 August 1938. Apart from the record-breaking machine (V-1) only three prototypes were built with the set-back cabin as the flight experience with the Bf 209 proved rather negative. Initially a DB 601 V-10 experimental engine was installed, later the DB 603A was envisaged. The Me 209 V-4 with longer wings was to show off its advantages as a military machine, but plans for a major series production were abandoned

Aircraft Type:	Me 209 A-2 (Project)
Purpose:	Fighter and fighter-bomber
Crew:	One
Engine plant:	1 x Jumo 213E (1508 kW, 2050 hp)
Wingspan:	10.94 m
Length:	9.74 m
Height:	4 m
Wing area:	17.2 sq.m
Top speeds:	645 kms/hr (low level), 695 kms/hr at 6,000 m altitude
Landing speed:	140 kms/hr
Rate of climb to 6000 m:	Unknown
Weight empty:	3350 kgs
All-up weight:	4075 kgs
Service ceiling:	11,500 m (estimated)
Range:	600 kms (estimated)
Armament:	1 x MK 108 or 1 x Mk 103 (mechanised gun), 2 x MG 151/20

The development of the Me 209, thought of as the successor to the Bf 109, was dropped in favour of the Bf 109 H-0.

in September 1938. In the spring of 1943 Messerschmitt attempted to score some points at RLM with a "new Me 209", but in the end the Fw 190 D-9 made all the running. Despite passable performances of the Me 209 HV5 (SP+LI) fitted with a DB 603, all efforts were also in vain on this occasion. The first of the "new Me 209" was to serve as a prototype for the A-1 series, the second for the A-2, but the design lost favour to the Bf 109 H-0. The Me 209 HV-6 with a Jumo 213E engine was therefore never built.

Head-on view of an Me 209 on the airfield at Augsburg.

Bf (Me) 210

The Messerschmitt project P 1060 was to be developed within the shortest time possible not only as a heavy fighter against targets in the air, but also as a "destroyer capable of dive-bombing" ground targets. In the summer of 1937, that is to say at a time when the Bf 110 was still undergoing testing, the RLM was already thinking in terms of a successor to the planned Bf 110 Destroyer. After the final plans and the Bf 210 prototype had been completed within only twelve months, Dr Hermann Wurster flew the Bf 210 V-1 (D-AABF) on 5 September 1939. Because stability around the longitudinal axis, the elevators and the balance of the aircraft came into question, the flight characteristics were not of the best. Fuselage

Aircraft Type:	Bf 210 A-1
Purpose:	Destroyer
Crew:	Two
Engine plant:	2 x DB 601 F (each 875-994 kW, 1100-1350 hp)
Wingspan:	16.34 m
Length:	11.2 m
Height:	3.7 m
Wing area:	36.2 sq.m
Top speeds:	580 kms/hr at 6000 m altitude, 480 kms/hr (low level)
Landing speed:	180 kms/hr
Rate of climb to 6000 m:	13 mins
Weight empty:	7070 kgs
All-up weight:	9460 kgs
Service ceiling:	8900 m
Range:	1730 kms
Armament:	2 x MG 151/20, 2 x MG 17, 2 x FSDL 131 with MG 131

The (Bf) Me 210 V-1 had a twin rudder system.

and wings, which initially had no leading edge slats, had to be intensively modified, and the wing profile required changes, to mention only the major weaknesses. The production plan, to begin with the first 1,000 Bf 210 A-1 from early 1941, was therefore deferred to the end of the year. The first two series machines (Bf 210 A-1) were delivered in July 1941. Fast-bomber squadron 210 received its first 16 machines in November. By March 1942 fewer than 80 Bf 210 had come off the production lines, another 205 were under construction at that time.

Meanwhile a number of accidents resulted in the production of the Bf 210 being terminally halted on 9 March 1942. In order that the knowledge should not have been in vain, the bulk of the surviving Bf 210 aircraft were worked on to produce, in the shape of the Me 410, a thoroughly efficient and reliable machine.

The Me 210 development was broken off due to serious problems of stability.

Me 261

The Messerschmitt project (P) 1062 was to have been a long-range courier and communications aircraft. The RLM required a range of up to 11,000 kms in order to reach the Japanese ally. The two-engined Me 261 was the result. The two experimental aircraft received two DB 606-double engines each. The more powerful DB 610 double-motor was planned for the third. Karl Baur piloted the Me 261 V-1 (Works Nr 2445, BJ+CP) on its maiden flight on 23 December 1941. The pure flight characteristics were thoroughly acceptable, but for a long time problems persisted with the retractable undercarriage. The experimental Me 261 V-2 and V-3 followed in October 1942. The planned series of 20 to 30 machines never came to fruition despite an oral assurance to the contrary by RLM. Apart from the use as a courier aircraft it was also planned to use the machine for long-range reconnaissance and as a long-range transport. Only the second prototype survived the war, albeit in a damaged condition.

Aircraft Type:	Me 261 V-2
Purpose:	Long range courier aircraft
Crew:	Three to four
Engine plant:	2 x DB 606 A/B (each 1986 kW, 2700 hp)
Wingspan:	26.87 m
Length:	16.68 m
Height:	4.72 m
Wing area:	85 sq.m
Top speed:	585 kms/hr at 3000 m altitude
Landing speed:	125 kms/hr
Rate of climb to 4000 m:	21 mins
Weight empty:	10500 kgs
All-up weight:	29000 kgs
Service ceiling:	11800 m
Range:	13,200 kms no armament

During trials of the Me 261 many crash-landings occurred.

Only one of three Me 261 survived the war to be captured in a damaged condition by US forces.

Me 262 Experimental Aircraft

The twin-turbine jet fighter Me 262 A-1a transformed the face of the air war within a year. All deadlines were put back on account of the numerous problems with the new kind of engine. From the Me P 1065 project of a "pursuit fighter" came initially the Me 262 V-1 (PC+UA) fitted with a single Jumo 210G with variable pitch propellor which flew for the first time on 18 April 1941. The second "maiden flight", this time with two BMW P 3302 turbines and a piston engine to be on the safe side, followed on 25 March 1942. After the BMW turbines had failed to impress, the Me 262 V-3 was the first machine to receive two Jumo 004 experimental plant. This aircraft was flown successfully on 17 July 1942 by Fritz Wendel. Apart from the ten experimental aircraft of which six were lost to mishaps or crashed, 15

Aircraft Type:	Me P 1065
Purpose:	Jet fighter (experimental machine)
Crew:	One
Engine plant:	2 x BMW P 3304 (each 4.41 kN, 450 hp)
Wingspan:	12.35 m
Length:	10.6 m
Height:	2.8 m
Wing area:	20 sq.m
Top speeds:	855 kms/hr at 6000 m altitude, 785 kms/hr (low level)
Landing speed:	145 kms/hr
Rate of climb to 6,000 m:	Altitude, 15 mins
Weight empty:	2900 kgs
All-up weight:	4500 kgs
Service ceiling:	8000+ m
Range:	1200 kms
Armament:	3 x MG 151 (planned)

nil-series, Me 262 S-1 to 15 were built. From 3 January 1945 the only surviving machines of the nil-series, V-9 and V-10, were included in the new prototype series Me 262 V-1 to V-8/V-11 and V-12 taken from the running production and used for testing purposes.

The early experimental versions of the Me 262 had no nose wheel.

Me 262 A-1

After it could be forseen that the conclusion of the Me 262 development was approaching, the existing orders were amended on 25 May 1943 and for the first time 100 series aircraft ordered for tactical tests as jet fighters. The experience with the nil-series had already shown that within a short period the Luftwaffe would have available to it a superior operational machine. From the end of 1943, after statements from his entourage, Adolf Hitler saw the aircraft not as a fighter, but from the summer of 1944 principally as a "Blitz-bomber" to defend against the Allied invasion. Not until early in 1945 did this attitude change basically, and from then on the fighter-version dominated. Apart from the standard Me 262 A-1a, only the "auxiliary bomber" (A-1/Bo) and the Me 262 A-1a/R1 armed with R4M rockets appeared in mentionable numbers for operations. By the war's end the bad-weather fighter A-1a/U1, and the mixed-armament jet were still prototypes at the development stage. By 19 April 1945 according to Messerschmitt documentation 1,433 Me 262 had come off the assembly line, more than 500 were being built. Over 611 were damaged or destroyed before they reached the operational units: 114 of these were repaired and later delivered.

Aircraft Type:	Me 262 A-1a
Purpose:	Fighter
Crew:	One
Engine plant:	2 x Jumo 004 B-1/B-2 (each 8.8 kN, 900 hp)
Wingspan:	12.65 m
Length:	10.61 m
Height:	2.85 m
Wing area:	21.7 sq.m
Top speeds:	880 kms/hr at 9000 m altitude, 640 kms/hr at 6,000 m
Landing speed:	175 kms/hr
Rate of climb to 6000 m:	6.8 mins
Weight empty:	4365 kgs
All-up weight:	7100 kgs
Service ceiling:	11,450 m
Range:	880 kms
Armament:	4 x MK 108

(Above) Many mishaps occurred even during the testing of the Me 262 nil-series.
(Below) Towards the end of the war US forces captured numerous Me 262 A-1 and A-2 machines along the Reich autobahns.

Me 262 A-1a/U4 (E-1) with Mk 214 A

The desire to destroy a four-engined bomber with every round fired led to the fitting of heavy aircraft cannons even aboard the Me 262. This was ordered by Hitler on 4 November 1944. The nose of a new "Bomber-formation destroyer", the Me 262 A-1a/U4, was set up as a 1:1 wooden mock-up, the plans were delivered by 25 January 1945. That month firing tests were carried out with the MK 214. At Lechfeld on 11 March 1945 the first fuselage tip was fitted with the heavy MK 214 AV2. The first prototype, Me 262 A-1a (Works Nr 111 899) was tested first on the ground, firing 47 rounds. 81 more were fired in flight. There were occasional blockages and by 9 April 1945 it had still not been possible to make the cannon reliable. At the beginning of April 1945 the second prototype (Works Nr 170 083) received

Aircraft Type:	Me 262 A-1a/U4
Purpose:	"Bomber formation destroyer"
Crew:	One
Engine plant:	2 x Jumo 004 B-1/B-2 (each 8.8 kN, 900 hp)
Wingspan:	12.65 m
Length:	13.4 m
Height:	2.85 m
Wing area:	21.7 sq.m
Top speed:	840 kms/hr at 6,000 m altitude
Cruising speed:	735 kms/hr
Landing speed:	180 kms/hr
Rate of climb to 6,000 m:	7 mins
Weight empty:	4000 kgs
All-up weight:	6900 kgs
Service ceiling:	11,000 m
Range:	900 kms
Armament:	1 x Mk 214 AV2 and AV3

the MK 214 AV3 at Lechfeld. On 16 April 1945 Major Herget flew two unsuccessful sorties in which the weapon failed to function. The Me 262 E-1 series was then abandoned.

Equipping the Me 262 A-1a with a very heavy cannon did not have the success hoped for.

Me 262A-1a/U3 and A5

Aircraft Type:	Me 262A-1a/U3
Purpose:	Short-range reconnaissance
Crew:	One
Engine plant:	2 x Jumo 004 B-1/B-2 (each 8.8 kN, 900 hp)
Wingspan:	12.65 m
Length:	10.61 m
Height:	2.85 m
Wing area:	21.7 sq.m
Top speed:	870 kms/hr at 6,000 m altitude
Cruising speed:	750 kms/hr
Landing speed:	175 kms/hr
Rate of climb to 6000 m:	6.8 mins
Weight empty:	4365 kgs
All-up weight:	7000 kgs
Service ceiling:	11,450 m
Range:	1200 km (max)
Armament:	1 x Mk 108 (experimental fitment)

The development of a fast reconnaissance machine based on the Me 262 A-1a began in September 1941. Initially the RLM ordered an unarmed jet reconnaissance aircraft with film camera (Rb). The work took longer than planned because the RLM could not decide on the final equipment. Therefore it was not until August 1944 that an "auxiliary reconnaissance machine", the Me 262 A-1a/U3 (Works Nr 170 006), made its debut. In October 1944 work began on setting up the Me 262 short-range reconnaissance commando Brunegg and a month later the group was equipped. The Me 262A-1a/U3 flown from there were fitted with two film cameras in the nose. Only one prototype, corresponding closely to the planned series run of jet reconnaissance machines, the Me 262A-5, was tested, from mid-December 1944. The planned A-5 run was not realized on account of the war situation and so conversions of existing models continued. By 30 April 1945 a total of 57 "auxiliary reconnaissance" machines had been turned out.

Only the use of fast jet aircraft such as the Me 262A-1/U3 could be relied upon at the beginning of 1945 for reliable short-range reconnaissance.

Me 262 A-2 and A-2/U2

Aircraft Type:	Me 262 A-2a/U2
Purpose:	Lotfebomber
Crew:	Two
Engine plant:	2 x Jumo 004 B-1/B-2 (each 8.8 kN, 900 hp)
Wingspan:	12.51 m (another source says 12.65 m)
Length:	10.6 m
Height:	2.85 m
Wing area:	21.7 sq.m
Top speeds:	655 kms/hr at 3000 m altitude, 500 kms/hr at 400 m altitude
Landing speed:	175 kms/hr
Rate of climb to 6000 m:	7.1 mins
Weight empty:	4250 kgs
All-up weight:	7200 kgs
Service ceiling:	11,000 m
Range:	750 kms close to the ground
Armament:	2 x Mk 108 (planned)

Besides its role as a fighter, at the beginning of 1943 the Me 262 was already being seen as a fast fighter-bomber. In May 1944 an Me 262 A-1a received two ETC 503's below the fuselage forward. On 22 July 1944 the construction specifications for the Me 262 A-2a "Blitz-bomber" were completed. Mid-November 1944 the tactical trials finished. The machines were delivered principally to KG 51 "Edelweiss" for operations over the Western Front as were the "Blitz-bombers" of the Me 262 A-1a/Bo conversions. To improve bombing accuracy the low-level catapult installation (TSA) was fitted and tried out at the end of 1944. A special version was the two-seater Me 262 A-2a/U2. The first prototype (Works Nr. 110484) flew eleven times before the end of 1944, including bombing with use of the Lotfe-bombsight operated by the bomb-aimer stretched out in the nose of the aircraft. By 30 March 1945 the second Me 262 A-2a/U2 had made ten flights. This machine crashed at Marburg/Lahn shortly before the war ended and fell into the hands of US forces.

This "auxiliary bomber" Me 262 A-1a/Bo at Lechfeld was used for trials of the Me 262 A as a "Blitzbomber".

Me 262 B-1

For the training or conversion of pilots to the Me 262 A-1a a purpose-built training aircraft was needed. The first such machine, converted from a series-type Me 262 A-1a at Blohm & Voss, Wenzendorf, was Works Nr 130 010 (VI+AJ). The machine was tested at Rechlin in August 1944. In July 1944 seven single-seaters were already in series conversion to training aircraft. The planning in the summer of 1944 foresaw 65 machines. Wenzendorf works was hit by a heavy air raid on 27 November 1944. By 30 November Messerschmitt had delivered 31 airframes there, and of these a number were destroyed. After the damage was repaired at the beginning of 1945 Wenzendorf Works was bombed again forcing the partial removal of the aircraft factory to the aerodrome at Stade. The presumed last Me 262 B-1a was flown as BV37. It is thought that by 18 April 1945 Blohm & Voss had turned out 18 Me 262 B-1 aircraft from delivered A-1a airframes. About 17 other aircraft or parts of them were lost to bomb damage.

Aircraft Type:	Me 262 B-1
Purpose:	Trainer
Crew:	Two
Engine plant:	2 x Jumo 004 B-1/B-2 (each 8.8 kN, 900 hp)
Wingspan:	12.65 m
Length:	10.61 m
Height:	2.85 m
Wing area:	21.7 sq.m.
Top speed:	870 kms/hr at 6000 m altitude
Cruising speed:	750 kms/hr
Landing speed:	175 kms/hr
Rate of climb to 6000 m:	Altitude, 6.8 mins
Weight empty:	4365 kgs
All-up weight:	6350 kgs
Service ceiling:	11,300 m
Range:	750 kms
Armament:	Up to 4 x MK 108

This dual seater (B-1a) was amongst the Me 262 aircraft captured by US forces.

Me 262 B-1a/U1 and B-2 (NJ)

Aircraft Type:	Me 262 B-2
Purpose:	Night fighter
Crew:	Two
Engine plant:	2 x Jumo 004 B-1/B-2 (each 8.8 kN, 900 hp)
Wingspan:	12.65 m
Length:	10.61 m
Height:	2.85 m
Wing surface:	21.7 sq.m
Top speed:	810 kms/hr at 6000 m altitude
Cruising speed:	730 kms/hr
Landing speed:	180 kms/hr
Rate of climb to 6000 m:	7.8 mins
Weight empty:	4780 kgs
All-up weight:	7980 kgs
Service ceiling:	11,450 m
Range:	1000 kms
Armament:	2 to 4 x MK 108

Two-seater training aircraft provided the ideal springboard for the creation of an "auxiliary night fighter" (B-1a/U1) and the improved series (B-2a). The auxiliary version originated from the "Project Transfer Conversion Training Aircraft Stage I" of 5 October 1944. The two-seater was to receive an FuG 350 ZC-Naxos-installation and the FuG 16 ZY. The need to carry two crew resulted in a rearrangement of the fuel tanks. The machines were attached to night-fighter squadron 10./NJG 11 and obtained 50 confirmed victories. The slightly lengthened Me 262 B-2 was due to make its appearance at the beginning of 1945, production being planned for the autumn of 1944, but as a result of the war situation it would seem that none was completed. The further developments began instead at the beginning of 1945, the "night fighter with HeS 011 jet turbines" or the "three-seater night fighter with HeS 011 engines" (27 March 1945)

were planned at first to have Heinkel turbines and the new FuG 240 radar. The development ended in May 1945 with the "night fighter with PTL drive". None of the experimental versions were built.

The Me 262 B-1a/U1 was used in limited numbers as night fighter over northern Germany with 10./NJ 11.

Me 262 C-1a

As the tactical range of the Me 163 was insufficient at well under 100 kms, in 1943 Messerschmitt designed a more efficient interceptor-fighter, the "Interceptor I". This would have a range of 745 kms and be able to stay up for a good 40 minutes. From this emerged the "Homeland Protector". The first and only prototype, the Me 262 C-1a (Works Nr 130 186) was fitted with a rocket motor (HWK 109-509 A-2) in the tail in August 1944. Various kinds of damage to the complicated additional motor, the supply lines and tanks led to numerous visits to the repairs hangar. The Lechfeld technicians finally managed to get the rocket motor functioning correctly on the stand on 22 February 1945. This time, fast regulation of the HWK rocket motor was achieved and the first rocket-assisted ascent took place on 27 February 1945. Two more take-offs were made by 19 March 1945, the fourth was aborted. Three days later the prototype was damaged by Allied low-level air attack. The repair was no longer possible in April 1945 and so the development was terminated.

Aircraft Type:	Me 262 C-1a
Purpose:	Protection of local industrial installations
Crew:	One
Engine plant:	2 x Jumo 004 B-1/B-2 (each 8.8 kN, 900 hp) and 1 x HWK 109-509 A-2 1 (16.7 kN, 700 hp)
Wingspan:	12.65 m
Length:	10.61 m
Height:	2.85 m
Wing area:	21.7 sq.m
Top speed:	950 kms/hr at 10,000 m altitude
Cruising speed:	880 kms/hr at 12,000 m
Landing speed:	175 kms/hr
Rate of climb to 10,000 m:	Altitude
Weight empty:	4440 kgs
All-up weight:	7160 kgs
Service ceiling:	13,500 m
Range:	400 kms
Armament:	4 x MK 108 (planned)

The "Homeland Protector I", the Me 262 C-1a was still far from operational at the beginning of 1945.

Me 262 C-2b

Aircraft Type:	Me 262 C-2b
Purpose:	"Homeland Protector"
Crew:	One
Engine plant:	2 x BMW 003R (each 12,25 kN, 1250 kp-800 kp and 450 kp rocket thrust)
Wingspan:	12.65 m
Length:	10.61 m
Height:	2.85 m
Wing area:	21.7 sq.m
Top speed:	870 kms/hr at 6000 m altitude
Cruising speed:	750 kms/hr
Landing speed:	170 kms/hr
Rate of climb to 12,000 m:	3.9 mins
Weight empty:	4975 kgs
All-up weight:	7100 kgs
Service ceiling:	16,000 m
Range:	850 kms
Armament:	4 x MK 108 (planned)

The development of the Me 262 "Interceptor II", a fighter for local protection with two BMW 003 R engines was begun in 1943. The transfer of the project on 4 September 1943 laid the groundwork for another TLR fighter, the Me 262 C-2b. A rocket aggregate (BMW 109-718) was added to each BMW 003 to provide a fast ascent to over 10,000 metres altitude. In June 1944 it was decided to build two prototypes. The first experimental aircraft intended for the conversion (Works Nr 170 074) arrived at Lechfeld on 20 December 1944. As a result of numerous technical problems, including one of the rocket aggregates exploding, the machine was never clear for take-off in subsequent weeks. In March 1945 the first standing trials were accomplished without premature breakdowns. Karl Baur flew the maiden TLR-flight on 26 March 1945. The second and last flight followed three days later. Since the propulsive system was still far from series readiness, the development of the Me 262 C-2b was broken off on 30 March 1945. The conversion of the second prototype (Works Nr 170 272) was also abandoned.

The complicated engine prevented a successful conclusion to testing of the Me 262 C-2b.

Me 262-HG I to HG III

Aircraft Type:	Me 262 high speed version (HG) II
Purpose:	Experimental aircraft
Crew:	One
Engine plant:	2 x Jumo 004 C-1 (13.8 kN, 1420 kp planned)
Wingspan:	12.16 m
Length:	10.61 m
Height:	2.85 m
Wing area:	24.8 sq.m
Top speeds:	1050 kms/hr (low level), 1100 kms/hr at 6000 altitude
Landing speed:	180 kms/hr
Rate of climb:	Not known
Weight empty:	4450 kgs
All-up weight:	7750 kgs
Service ceiling:	12,000 kgs
Range:	1000 kms
Armament:	4 x MK 108 (planned)

From the beginning of 1940 Messerschmitt took a keen interest in swept-wing development. In April 1941 RLM decided to try out the later Me 262's with a 35° swept-back wing to improve performance. The development was planned for three stages. From 1 October 1944 the Me 262 V-9 (Works Nr 130 004 VI+AD) was given a streamlined cabin cover, the "racing cockpit", so as to provide for swept elevators and a larger rudder unit. The following stage, HG II, was to have been tried experimentally with the Me 262 A-1a (Works Nr 111 538). Besides the former changes a 25° swept-wing was proposed. This machine was wrecked in March 1945 as the runway. Stage III, involving a 45° swept-wing and more powerful engine plant to provide the machine with a top speed of over 1000 kms/hr was also not realised. Apart from the future standard fighter in the variant HG III, above all the coming night-fighter versions were to be given swept wings and HeS 011 turbines integral in the wing roots.

The converted Me 262 (VI+AD) was the first prototype for the high-speed fighter (HG I).

Me 263 (Ju 248)

The Me 263 was a much improved Me 163 B-1. The Me 263, the further development of which was passed to Junkers as Ju 248 by the RLM, differed from its fore-runners principally in having a retractable undercarriage and a longer fuselage. This provided enough room for the rocket unit with two combustion chambers. On 8 February 1945 the Ju 248 V-1 (DV+PA) glider had a towed flight. 13 more flights followed up to 19 February. Because certain parts for the new rocket motor had not been delivered, testing at Dessau was discontinued. On 24 April 1945 the heavily damaged Ju 248 V-1 was captured by US forces.

Aircraft Type:	Me 263 (Ju 248)
Purpose:	Protection local installations
Crew:	One
Engine plant:	1 x HWK 109 509C (19.6 kN, 2000 kp)
Wingspan:	9.5 m
Length:	7.88 m
Height:	3.0 m
Wing area:	17.9 sq.m
Top speeds:	990 kms/hr at 10,000 m altitude, 700 kms/hr (low level)
Landing speed:	170 kms/hr
Rate of climb to 10,000 m:	3 mins
Weight empty:	3200 kgs
All-up weight:	5300 kgs
Service ceiling:	15,000 m
Range:	160 kms
Armament:	2 to 4 MK 108

Wind tunnel model of the Me 263 which was developed further as the Ju 248.

The wooden mock-up of the Ju 248 at Junkers.

Me 264

In the summer of 1940 OKM (Naval High Command) ordered an efficient four-engined long-range bomber with heavy defensive armament. The plans for this bomber/reconnaissance aircraft, the later Me 264, were almost completed by November 1941. In May 1942 RLM ordered a small series run of 30 Me 264 in addition to the five experimental aircraft. On 23 December 1942 Karl Baur flew the unarmed Me 264 V-1 prototype (RE+EN) at Lechfeld. One technical problem followed another and the overall development was delayed by frequent stays in the repair hangar. On 23 March 1943 Me 264 V-1 was seriously damaged while landing. Long repairs ensued. The experimental unit was then tested with mock-ups of future armament to establish whether they changed the behaviour of the aircraft in flight. The initially planned two rotatable turrets and two fixed turrets in the rear engine covers were not installed. Shortly

afterwards all work was abandoned. On 18 July 1944 the only prototype became the victim of an Allied air raid at Memmingen.

The only completed Me 264 with Imo 211 J motors.

Aircraft Type:	Me 264 V-1
Purpose:	Extreme long-range bomber (prototype)
Crew:	Five to seven
Engine plant:	4 x Jumo 211J (each 1030 kN, 1400 hp)
Wingspan:	38.9 m
Length:	21.33 m
Height:	4.28 m
Wing area:	124.3m sq m
Top speeds:	545 kms/hr at 8000 m altitude, 490 kms/hr (low level)
Landing speed:	160 kms/hr
Rate of climb to 6000 m:	42 mins
Weight empty:	20,500 kgs
All-up weight:	56,000 kgs
Service ceiling:	10,300 ms
Range:	13,500 kms

Me 264/6m

Ideas of flying operations against targets in the United States or over the Arabian area required a greater performance than that offered by the four-engined Me 264. This would be achieved by lengthening the wings and fitting six of the most powerful Jumo engines possible. The first provisional drawings were finished on 16 February 1942. The later plans envisaged the future addition of a motor segment alongside the fuselage. According to the planning the machine would have three rotatable turrets for 20-cm weapons on the upper and lower fuselage, an MG 131 V rear turret and another weapons position below the cabin. Apart from the six-motor version, in the spring of 1944 variants with swept-back wings and up to eight piston motors were designed. All these plans, and the installation of a steam turbine and jet engines as supplementary propulsion were no more than projects.

Aircraft Type:	Me 264/6m
Purpose:	Long range bomber
Crew:	Five to seven
Engine plant:	6 x BMW 801E (each 1287 kW, 1750 hp)
Wingspan:	47.5 m
Length:	25.5 m
Height:	4.3 m
Wing area:	170 sq.m
Top speed:	630 kms/hr
Cruising speed:	380 kms/hr
Landing speed:	153 kms/hr
Rate of climb:	Unknown
Weight empty:	31,000 kgs
All-up weight:	75,000 kgs
Service ceiling:	9,500 m
Range:	14,700 kms (highest calculated)
Armament:	Up to 10 MG 151/20 and 1 MG 131V

Model of the 6-engined version of the Me 264 as a strategic bomber.

Me 309

As a more efficient successor to the Bf 109 G Messerschmitt suggested to the RLM the Me 309 powered by a DB 603. The armament would consist of up to seven very heavy MG and MK's. Work on the single seater fighter began in December 1941. Development procedures proved complicated because the fuselage structure was totally different from that of the Bf 109. Not until 18 July 1942 could Karl Baur make the maiden flight with the Me 309 (GE+CU). After the first three experimental aircraft, the open question about the engine caused delays in the completion about the rest of the run. Moreover the handling of the Me 309 V-1 proved more difficult than that of the Bf 109 G-6. In December 1942 the Me 309 was held back in favour of the Fw 190 D-9. The last machine, Me 309 V-3 (CA+NK) was lost in February 1943. On 20 May 1943 the development was halted since the introduction of the Me 262 was imminent.

Aircraft Type:	Me 309
Purpose:	Heavy day-fighter
Crew:	One
Engine plant:	1 x DB 603G (1066-1287 kW, 1450-1750 hp)
Wingspan:	11 m
Length:	9.46 m
Height:	3.9 m
Wing area:	15.8 sq.m
Top speeds:	775 kms/hr at 10,000m altitude, 650 kms/hr (low level)
Landing speed:	150 kms/hr
Rate of climb to 8,000 m:	10.1 min
Weight empty:	3525 kgs
All-up weight:	4250 kgs
Service ceiling:	12,000 m
Range:	1200 kms
Armament:	1 x MK 108 cannon, up to 6 x MG 151/20 and 2 MG 131 (wings/fuselage)

In view of jet alternatives, the Me 309 failed to meet expectations.

The Me 309 V-1, here with altered rudder unit, was damaged in an air attack.

Me 321 "Gigant"

Aircraft Type:	Me 321 B-1
Purpose:	Transport glider
Crew:	Two to three
Take-off Engine plant:	Up to 8 x HWK 109-501 (each 14.7 kN, 1500 hp)
Wingspan:	55 m
Length:	28.15 m
Height:	10.5 m
Wing area:	300.5 sq.m
Angle of glide:	1:16.
Towing speed:	230 kms/hr
Landing speed:	115 kms/hr
Weight empty:	12.1 tonnes
All-up weight:	30 tonnes
Service ceiling:	2500 m
Armament:	6 to 17 MG 34 or MG 15

The requirement for a major air transport capacity became of ever greater importance in a modern war. From the late summer of 1940 a heavy transport glider was first mooted. Work on construction began in November 1940, the first flight followed on 25 February 1941. The designation was initially Me 321 Warschau ("Warsaw"). In 1941 work was done on the glider Me 263 and then again on the Me 321; by August 1941 200 of the giant transport gliders were built at Leipheim and Obertraubling. The Me 321A-1 was a transport

Approach of an Me 321 "Gigant" with landing flaps deployed.

Me 321 "Gigant"

glider with a disposable undercarriage. Mostly He 111 Z-1 but occasionally also Ju 90's acted as the tug aircraft. The first tow of the Me 321 (W4+SJ) by an He 111 Z-1 took place on 22 August 1941. On 29 September the tow was tried for the first time with two He 111, later experimentally by three Bf 110C. Thanks to this large glider it was possible to transport cumbersome goods, or important material in large quantities by air, but because of its size there were frequent problems under tow in the air and also on the ground so that a motorised version, the Me 323 with six engines, was built instead.

To assist take-off, up to eight disposable booster rockets could be carried under the wings of the Me 321.

Me 323 C

During the trials of the Me 321 in March 1941 it became clear that flying huge transport gliders was too complicated. Messerschmitt therefore suggested motorising the "Gigant", and in April that year provided the RLM with his plans. Shortly afterwards an Me 321 was given four Gnome and Rhone 14N radial motors at Obertraubling and flew for the first time on 21 April 1941 as the Me 323 AV1. The second four-engined version was designated Me 323 C and tested on 20 January 1942. The hold could accommodate one 22-tonne or two 9-tonne panzers, or 175 soldiers with full equipment in the fuselage and inner wings. Four radial engines proved short on power for this payload over long distances, however. For this reason Messerschmitt turned to version D, which had six instead of four engines.

Aircraft Type:	Me 323 C
Purpose:	Heavy cargo carrier
Crew:	Four
Engine plant:	4 x Gnome & Rhone 14 N (each 868-691 kW, 940-119 hp)
Wingspan:	55 m
Length:	28.15 m
Height:	10.5 m
Wing area:	300 sq.m
Top speed:	265 kms/hr
Cruising speed:	240 kms/hr
Landing speed:	165 kms/hr
Rate of climb:	Unknown
Weight empty:	19 tonnes
All-up weight:	41 tonnes
Service ceiling:	4,000 m
Range:	650+ kms
Armament:	6 to 10 MG 34 or MG 15

Four radial engines for the Me 323 C proved too few.

Me 323 D-1 to E-1

The Me 323 BV-1 was the first experimental unit with six engines. This was followed by the prototypes Me 323 V-2 to V-12 which provided experience for the future Me 323 D-1, the production of which began in July 1942. As a series, various differing motorised variants followed the "Dora", the first being the D-1 with "Bloch" engines and variable pitch "Ratier" propellors. The D-2 had six "Leo" motors with fixed, two-blade "Heine" wooden propellors, from the D-6 these were replaced by the "Ratiers". In case of emergency these engines were interchangeable one for another. The machines were of braced high-wing design and of mixed material construction. The fuselage and wings were of robust steel tubing. Me 323 V-13 and V-15 flew as prototypes for the E-1 version. The D-version had more armament with several rotating turrets and weapons positions with the MG 151/20 and MG 131. The

Aircraft Type:	Me 323 D-1
Purpose:	Heavy cargo carrier
Crew:	Two to three
Engine plant:	6 Bloch 175 with "Ratier" airscrews
Wingspan:	55.24 m
Length:	28.25 m
Height:	10.2 m
Wing area:	300.5 sq.m
Top speed:	300 kms/hr
Cruising speed:	250 kms/hr
Landing speed:	130 kms/hr
Rate of climb to 2000 m:	17 mins
Weight empty:	25 tonnes+
All-up weight:	44 tonnes+
Service ceiling:	4,500 m
Range:	950 kms at 4,000 m altitude
Armament:	2 x MG 151/20, 8 to 10 MG 15 and MG 131

The Me 323 could carry cumbersome cargo to the size of a large lorry.

This photograph taken near the huge loading doors emphasises the size of the Me 323.

planned Me 323 F to H versions would have had more power, but even the fitting of Jumo 211F, the DB 603 or even a more powerful engine plant such as the Gnome and Rhone 14R/A-5 would not have provided a real improvement in flight performance. The F-series experimental aircraft Me 323 V-16 broke up on 30 September 1944 and was written off. The prototype for the G-series was to have been the V-17, which was not ready in time, and the same went for the H version. The use of other transporters such as the Ju 352 was more promising.

The Me 323 was an easy target for Allied fighters and destroyers on account of its great size.

Me 323 E-2 "Weapons Carrier"

A few machines were put together from existing Me 323 E-2 as "weapons carriers", E/WT for short. These were not transport aircraft but gunships intended to provide formations of Me 323's with great firepower to ward off Allied fighters and destroyers. Armament was up to four MG 151/20-EDL rotatable turrets on the upper fuselage, another in the nose and several 2-cm or 13-mm gun positions either side of the fuselage. All this required a crew of twenty. One of the prototypes was tested at Rechlin on 29 March 1944. Apart from a few prototypes the planned conversion of more machines fell by the wayside because the tactical experience was not satisfactory.

Aircraft Type:	Me 323 E-2/WT
Purpose:	Gunship escort for the Me 323
Crew:	About 20
Engine plant:	6 x Gnone and Rhone 14 N/RN (each 868-691 kW, 940-1190 hp)
Wingspan:	55.24 m
Length:	28.5 m
Height:	10.2 m
Wing area:	300.5 sq.m
Top speed:	295 kms/hr
Cruising speed:	250 kms/hr
Landing speed:	130 kms/hr
Rate of climb to 3,000 m:	17 mins
Weight empty:	28 tonnes
All-up weight:	43.6 tonnes
Service ceiling:	5,000 m
Range:	850 kms
Armament:	8 x MG 151/20 in HD 151/1 and ED 151 positions, 6 x M 131 in WL 131 positions

Despite its profusion of turrets for 20mm weapons the Me 323 E-2 gunship failed to impress as an escort for transport flights.

Me 328 A (Experimental aircraft)

The Me 328 A resulted from project Me P 1079. According to the offer in the spring of 1941 the machine was to be above all a light, single-seater fast bomber and reconnaissance aircraft with ramjet propulsion. In March 1942 Messerschmitt presented the RLM with further plans for the Me 328 A-1 series. The maiden flight of the Me 328 AV-1 was piloted by Karl Baur on 3 August 1942. In the late summer the AV-2 was clear to fly and tested as a glider at the end of the year. The AV-0 served only as a mock-up and for ground tests. The Me 328 was co-opted into the "Vulkan Programm" on 10 December 1942, its principal role being as a single seater fast bomber for coastal defence. On 30 October 1943 the AV-1 flew as a glider towed up to altitude by a conventional aircraft and released. The converted Me 328 AV-2 was at that time 96% ready for testing with two ramjets.

Aircraft Type:	Me 328 AV-1
Purpose:	(Experimental) fast bomber
Crew:	One
Engine plant:	None
Wingspan:	6.4 m
Length:	8.65 m
Height:	2.15 m
Wing area:	7.5 sq.m
Top speed:	620 kms/hr at 3000 m, 700 kms/hr (low level)
Landing speed:	165 kms/hr
Weight empty:	1510 kgs
All-up weight:	2890 kgs
Service ceiling:	5500+ m
Range:	600 kms
Armament:	None (planned 1 MG 151/20 or MK 108)

Meanwhile an airframe had been equipped experimentally with armament and underwent testing until November 1943. In March 1944 work on the aircraft was surprisingly cut back to the AV-10. Further development from now on concentrated on the Me 328 B.

The flight tests with the Me 328 A were made without an engine plant.

Me 328 B (Experimental aircraft)

Aircraft Type:	Me 328 B-1 (Project)
Purpose:	Light bomber
Crew:	One
Engine plant:	2 x Argus As 014 ram jets
Wingspan:	6.9 m
Length:	7.05 m
Height:	2.86 m
Wing area:	8.5-9.45 sq.m
Top speed:	700 kms/hr (low level), 610 kms/hr at 3000 m altitude
Landing speed:	185 kms/hr
Weight empty:	1510 kgs
All-up weight:	3240 kgs
Service ceiling:	5500 m
Range:	710 kms
Armament:	None

After the RLM had lost interest in producing a small single seater shipborne aircraft, Messerschmitt proposed instead the deployment of the Me 328 as a light fast bomber. A planning study dated 15 December 1942 foresaw the construction of 300 wooden aircraft. Production at the Jacob Schweyer GmbH would involve 20 experimental units and 280 pre-series and series machines. Work on the first two, Me 328 BV-1 and BV-2, was begun in March 1943 but the development was halted prematurely, and interest did not revive until early 1944. In March 1944 Me 328 BV-1 was clear to fly and from mid-August 1944 made several glider flights from the Do 217

K-03. The idea behind the resumed work was an "aircraft for special purposes". This meant a "suicide aircraft" (SO) in which the pilot would give his life by crashing it into an especially rewarding target.

For ease of assembly Messerschmitts selected ramjet propulsion for the Me 328 B.

Me 329

In direct competition with Dr Alexander Lippisch's project Li P 10, in March 1942 Messerschmitt handed to the RLM the plans for the Me 329 "Stuke-fighter" conceived by Dr Hermann Wurster. This would be a bomber but also multi-purpose aircraft of modern "flying wing" design. The machine was be fitted with either two DB 603 of the most powerful version possible or two Jumo 213 inverted-V motors. The top speed calculated by Messerschmitt was ideally at over 790 kms/hr and the range between 4,350 kms and almost 5,000 kms depending on the payload. Despite these outstanding characteristics, the production was called off after the RLM lost interest in it and from 1943 staked everything on two-engined jet fighters such as the Me 262 A-1a. All that remained was a 1:1 mock-up and comprehensive calculations.

Aircraft Type:	Me 329
Purpose:	(Experimental) multi-purpose bomber
Crew:	Two
Engine plant:	2 x DB 603B or Jumo 213 A/E
Wingspan:	17.5 m
Length:	8.55 m
Height:	4.75 m
Wing area:	62.7 sq.m
Top speed:	630 kms/hr (low level), 745 kms/hr at 7,000 m altitude
Landing speed:	150 kms/hr
Rate of climb to 6,000 m:	7.9 mins
Weight empty:	6950 kgs
All-up weight:	12,150 kgs
Service ceiling:	12,000 m
Range:	4450 kms
Armament:	4 x MG 151/20 or 2 x MK 103 and 1 FHL 131 as a remotely operated gun position

Only a full-size wooden mock-up of the Me 329 was ever made.

Me 410 (Experimental aircraft)

It was considered that a more efficient destroyer aircraft would result from lengthening the fuselage of the Me 401 by 80 cms, improving the wings and providing more powerful DB 603 engines. In July 1942 work was begun on the first conversions from the Me 210 groups. Once the standards insisted upon by the RLM had been met, the development was redesignated Me 410 from August 1942. The Me 210 (Works Nr 210 000 027 DI+NW) was the first prototype to fly with DB 603 engines. Me 210 V-17 (Works Nr 101, NE+BH) with a longer fuselage took to the air on a test flight in February 1942. With Me 410 V-1, therefore the renamed DI+BW, engine trials were continued and flights made to examine stability. Me 410 V-2, the former Bf 210 V-23, was used for trials of the engines and BK 5 cannon. Other experimental units were the Me 410 V-12, V-16 to 18, and the V-22.

Aircraft Type:	Me 410 V-1
Purpose:	(Experimental) destroyer
Crew:	One
Engine plant:	2 x DB 603A (each 772-883 kW, 1050-1200 hp)
Wingspan:	16.36 m
Length:	10.56 m
Height:	5.2 m
Wing area:	36.2 sq.m
Top speed:	500 kms/hr (low level)
Cruising speed:	640 kms/hr at 6,000 m altitude
Landing speed:	165 kms/hr
Rate of climb to 6,000 m altitude:	14.2 mins
Weight empty:	6,500 kgs
All-up weight:	10,900 kgs
Service ceiling:	11,100 m
Range:	1,450 kms
Armament:	2 x MG 151/20 and 2 x MG 17 (fixed), 2 x MG 131 in FDSL-B 131 (manoeuvrable)

Numerous Me 410's were built for various experimental purposes such as here the fitting of an FuG 200 radar.

Me 410 A-1 to A-3

The first series run, the Me 410 A-1, was a "fast fighting aircraft" with a payload of up to 1000 kgs, for example with two SD 500 bombs. From December 1942 about 130 Bf 210 were converted to Me 410 A-1, then brand new machines followed. Me 410 A-1/U1 flew as "auxiliary reconnaissance aircraft" armed with only two MG 151/20. A-1/U-2 was tested as an "auxiliary destroyer" with a WB 151 gun mount but without defensive armament. Two double-tubes for mortars were used operationally at ZG 1 squadron. Me 410 A-1/U4 had a BK 5 cannon. From version Me 410 A-2, a destroyer with six fixed weapons, amongst them two MK 103, the bomb retention gear was dropped. Also the A-2 was used in action as A-2/U4 with a BK 5 cannon. A-3 followed as a reconnaissance machine with film camera apparatus in the bomb bay. As A-3/U1, 25 aircraft were fitted with a GM-1 unit to improve performance.

Aircraft Type:	Me 410 A-1
Purpose:	Fast bomber
Crew:	Two
Engine plant:	2 x DB 603A (each 1177-1383 kW, 1600-1880 hp)
Wingspan:	16.36 m
Length:	10.56 m
Height:	5.2 m
Wing area:	36.2 sq.m
Top speed:	500 kms/hr (low level)
Cruising speed:	630 kms/hr at 8,000 m altitude
Landing speed:	165 kms/hr
Rate of climb to 6,000 m:	13 mins
Weight empty:	6500 kgs
All-up weight:	11,300 kgs
Service ceiling:	11,500 m
Range:	1350 kms
Armament:	2 x MG 151/20 and 2 MG 17 (fixed), 2 x MG 131 in FDSL-B 131 (manoeuvrable)

Very heavy weaponry as aboard the Mr 410A-1/U-4 proved inferior to machines with several MK 108s.

Me 410 B-1 to B-8

The Me 410 B-1 with two DB 603 G engines flew as a "fast fighting aircraft" and together with four fixed weapons could also carry up to a one-tonne bomb load. As with the Me 410 A-1, conversions U1 to U4 were available. On some of the Me 410 B-2 destroyers, two MK 103 were mounted – as with the A-2 – and four other fixed weapons in the nose. The usual conversions were always possible with the B-2. Nearly all other variants, generally the B-3, B-7 and B-8, were reconnaissance aircraft for day or night operations. The LT-Carrier B-5 did not show, the B-6, a "maritime destroyer" with FuG 200 only in limited numbers. The idea of fitting the Me 410 with a jet turbine below the fuselage in addition to the standard engine plant proved too complicated. Until production was halted in the summer of 1944, Messerschmitt and Dornier together turned out about 900 new aircraft. From the construction runs B-1 to B-3 about 350 machines were cut. About 280 Me 410 were manufactured from component parts of the Bf 210.

Aircraft Type:	Me 410 B-1
Purpose:	Fast bomber
Crew:	Two
Engine plant:	2 x DB 603 A/G (each 1177-1383 kW, 1600-1880 hp)
Wingspan:	16.35 m
Length:	12.56 m
Height:	5.21 m
Wing area:	36.2 sq.m
Top speed:	500 kms/hr (low level)
Landing speed:	1790 kms/hr
Rate of climb to 6,000 m:	10.7 mins
Weight empty:	7175 kgs
All-up weight:	11,350 kgs
Service ceiling:	9750 m
Range:	2400 kms
Armament:	2 x MG 151/20 and 2 x MG 17 (fixed), 2 x MG 131 in FDSL-B (manoeuvrable).

The Me 410 B sometimes provided good service as a reconnaissance aircraft or for the detection of Allied bombers until the beginning of 1945.

Me P 1100

To the ongoing development of an Me 262 with lengthened fuselage at the beginning of 1944, the complete specifications were ready by 22 March 1944. For the jet bomber based on the Me 262 A-2 a wooden partial mock-up for the cabin area was built. The fuselage was of the shell-construction method. The roomy cabin had the two crew in a staggered arrangement. The bomb bay could carry (up to two) one 1000 kg (and) or two 500-kg loads. In the first development stage defensive armament was not planned for since it was thought that the superior speed would be enough. It was recognised later that operations without armament would have severely limited tactical possibilities. For this reason it was planned to have three weapons installations which could be operated from the cabin. As a result of the war situation work on the P 1100 was abandoned and all efforts directed towards the Me 262 A-1 and A-2.

Aircraft Type:	Me P 1100 (First development stage)
Purpose:	Fast bomber
Crew:	Two
Engine plant:	2 x Jumo 004 C-1 (each 12.2 kN, 1250 hp)
Wingspan:	12.65 m
Length:	10.6 m
Height:	2.8 m
Wing area:	21.75 sq.m
Top speeds:	720 kms/hr (low level), 780 kms/hr at 6,000 m altitude
Landing speed:	165 kms/hr
Rate of climb to 5,000 m:	6.3 mins
Weight empty:	4100 kgs
All-up weight:	7,800 kgs
Service ceiling:	9,200 m
Range:	1250 kms
Armament:	None, but rotatable chassis planned for later

Only this mock-up of the cabin was made in the framework of the project P 1100 development.

Me P 1101

The aim of Project P 1101 was to develop a single-engined jet fighter faster and lighter than the Me 262 versions being introduced. The first design, dated 24 July 1944, had a turbine in the fuselage and two air intakes at the sides. Numerous other concepts were analysed before the project bureau settled for the P 1101. The machine was initially an unarmed "experimental aircraft". It was agreed in December 1944 that the future Heinkel HeS 011 A engine would be the most suitable for the design. The first prototype, the Me P 1101 V-1 was produced at the Oberbayrische Forschungsanstalt (Messerschmitt), Oberammergau. The prototype had reached an advanced stage but was fitted with only a wooden mock-up of the turbine for work on the engine cover when US forces arrived. The captured aircraft was dismantled and taken to the United States in the summer of 1945.

Aircraft Type:	Me P 1101
Purpose:	Experimental aircraft
Crew:	One
Engine plant:	1 x Jumo 004 B-2, Jumo 004 C-1 or HeS 011 A-0 (planned)
Wingspan:	8.08 m
Length:	8.92 m
Height:	3.72 m
Wing area:	13.6 sq.m
Top speed:	985 kms/hr at 7,000 m altitude
Cruising speed:	800 kms/hr at 8,000 m at altitude
Landing speed:	170 kms/hr
Rate of climb to 10,000 m:	9.5 mins
Weight empty:	2600 kgs
All-up weight:	4000 kgs
Service ceiling:	14,000 m
Range:	1500 kms
Armament:	None

The only Me P 1101 prototype was not finished as a result of the war situation.

Me P 1106

Project Me P 1106 worked out by Messerschmitt at the beginning of 1945 was intended to be a fast fighter. Engine plant would be the HeS 011 A-0 expected to be ready in the early summer that year. The design was a further development of the P 1101. The aim was to create a very fast and nimble machine with the least complications in production and materials. The single-seater would have a pressure cabin and two MK 108 in the nose. The carriage of all kinds of payload outside was theoretically possible. The design was submitted to the DVL in January 1945 where the specialists took the surprising view that the more costly P 1110 would definitely be superior to the Me P 1106 and declined to authorise further development.

Aircraft Type:	Me P 1106
Purpose:	Fighter (planned)
Crew:	One
Engine plant:	1 x HeS 011 A-1 (12.7 kN, 1300 kp)
Wingspan:	6.65 m
Length:	9.05 m
Height:	3.37 m
Wing surface:	13.17 sq.m
Top speed:	995 kms/hr at 7000 m altitude
Cruising speed:	850 kms/hr
Landing speed:	185 kms/hr
Rate of climb to 6,000 m:	Unknown
Weight empty:	2300 kgs
All-up weight:	4000 kgs
Service ceiling:	13,300 m
Range:	1600 kms
Armament:	2 x MK 108 (planned)

Drawing of the Messerschmitt Me P 1106 project (Backmann).

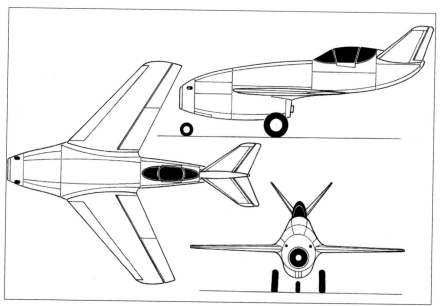

Me P 1110

Messerschmitt's project Me P 1110 originated in February 1945. This was a frequently modified design for a single-seater jet fighter. After their evaluation the DVL recommended enlarging the wings and revising the air intakes for the turbine built into the fuselage. The three fixed MK 108 in the nose remained unchanged. Even redesigning for the "duck-wing" style at cabin level was considered but rejected although this promised better lateral stability and good characteristics at slow speed. The project was still being worked on intensively at Oberammergau in March 1945. Mid-month various tests were made for the installation of heavy cannon, perhaps the Mk 112 of MK 214. The experience gained became the groundwork of the extremely progressive Messerschmitt project P 1112. After the war in Sweden, with plans from Messerschmitt, Saab built the J-32 "Lansen", which leaned heavily on the P-1110.

Aircraft Type:	Me P 1110
Purpose:	Fighter (Experimental aircraft)
Crew:	One
Engine plant:	1 x HeS 011 A-1 (12.7 kN, 1300 kp)
Wingspan:	8.25 m
Length:	10.35 m
Height:	3.2 m
Wing area:	15.85 sq.m
Top speeds:	900 kms/hr (low level), 1015 kms/hr at 7000 m altitude
Landing speed:	180 kms/hr
Rate of climb to 6000 m:	Unknown
Weight empty:	2800 kgs
All-up weight:	4300 kgs
Service ceiling:	12,500 m
Range:	1400 kms
Armament:	3 to 5 x MK 108

Drawing of the project-study Me P 1110, a single jet-engined fighter.

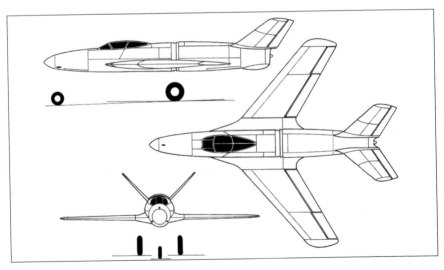

Me P 1112

Project P 1112 was among the last work done by Messerschmitt at the Oberbayrische Forschungsanstalt. The project commenced in the spring of 1945. The first drawings showing four slightly differing versions of the single-seater fighter were dated between 3 and 30 March 1945. The earlier variants have an all-metal mid-wing monoplane with retractable undercarriage. The end of the development, the P 112 S-2 version, had a modern V-tail unit which enabled the original wing area to be reduced from 22 sq.m. to only 19 sq.m. Shortly before, on 15 March 1945, work had begun on a full-size fuselage mock-up of the P 1112 at Oberammergau. At the beginning of April 1945 Messerschmitt handed in to Berlin the specifications of the new fighter driven by an HeS 011 A or B turbine. An assessment of the 1:1 mock-up was made on 8 April 1945. Shortly afterwards, on 29 April, US forces arrived at Oberammergau and terminated the work.

Aircraft Type:	Me P 1112 V-1
Purpose:	Fighter (planned experimental version)
Crew:	One
Engine plant:	1 x HeS 011 A-1 (12,7 kN, 1300 kp)
Wingspan:	8.75 m
Length:	8.25 m
Height:	3.6 m
Wing area:	19 sq.m.
Top speeds:	1000 kms/hr at 7000 m altitude, 940 kms/hr at 9000 m altitude
Landing speed:	165 kms/hr
Rate of climb:	Unknown
Weight empty:	2295 kgs
All-up weight:	4700 kgs
Service ceiling:	12500 m
Range:	1500 kms
Armament:	4 x MK 108

The progress on the Me P 1112 at the war's end went as far as this full-size partial mock-up at Oberammergau.

HA 100 "Triana"

Aircraft Type:	HA 100 F "Triana"
Purpose:	Trainer
Crew:	Two
Engine plant:	1 x Wright "Cyclone 7" (588 kW, 800 hp)
Wingspan:	10.4 m
Length:	8.87 m
Height:	3.05 m
Wing area:	17 sq.m
Top speed:	476 kms/hr
Cruising speed:	410 kms/hr
Landing speed and rate of climb:	Not known
Weight empty:	1700 kgs
All-up weight:	2450 kgs
Service ceiling:	9500 m
Range:	1000+ kms, unarmed

Cooperation between Messerschmitt and the Spanish firm Hispano Aviation (HA) began in the late summer of 1951. The development team in Spain began work first on a two-seater trainer, based on an official request the same year. The machine was intended for novices as well as progressing learners. The initial protoype HA 100 E flew for the first time on 10 December 1953 with a "Beta" engine. The second experimental unit was the HA 100 F. Both aircraft were manufactured by Hispano Aviation at Seville. They differed from each other by the motor covering, behind which sat either a radial motor of 330 kW (450 hp) or a more powerful one of 590 kW (900 hp). The series run of the all-metal low wing monoplane was to have received an Elizalde Sirio motor by ENMASA. After the bad experience with the "Beta" motor the HA 100 F was fitted with a Wright "Cyclone 7" with which it made its maiden flight in February 1955. As funds did not extend to the purchase of the American motors the series run of 40 aircraft was stopped.

The Ha 100 was the first aircraft to be designed by Messerschmitt after the war.

Checking over the HA 100 engine during the trials in Spain.

HA 200 and HA 220 "Saeta"

Aircraft Type:	HA 200 D/E
Purpose:	Trainer
Crew:	Two
Engine plant:	2 x Turbomeca "Marboré VI (each 4.7 kN, 480 hp)
Wingspan:	10.93 m
Length:	8.97 m
Height:	2.85 m
Wing area:	17.4 sq.m
Top speed:	690 kms/hr
Cruising speed:	580 kms/hr
Landing speed and rate of climb:	Unknown
Weight empty:	2020 kgs
All-up weight:	3600 kgs
Service ceiling:	12,500 m
Range:	1500 kms, no armament

The second development completed by Messerschmitt in Spain was the HA 200 "Pfeil". The two-seater jet trainer, for which components from the HA 100 were used in construction, flew for the first time on 12 August 1955. Apart from the training of novices and progressing learners, the aircraft was to be used for weapons training and reconnaissance flights. Professor Willy Messerschmitt, active in an advisory capacity, took the HA 100 framework and integrated two Turboméca "Marboré II" turbines into the nose in front of the cabin. In order to facilitate the export of the Fouga "Magister", France prohibited the delivery of turbines to Spain. The first of ten pre-series

aircraft therefore did not fly until 1961. In 1959 the Spanish Government awarded a contract for 30 HA 200 A. Five pre-series machines went as

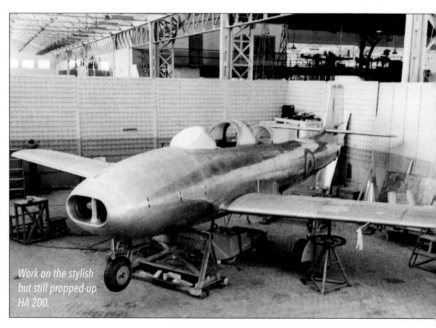

Work on the stylish but still propped-up HA 200.

HA 200 B to Egypt after being fitted with a 2-cm cannon. Between 1960 and 1965 the Egyptians manufactured 90 of the "Al Kahira" under licence. In Spain 55 the HA 200 D with more powerful engines, the HA 200 E and the HA 220 fighter-bomber followed.

The HA 200 was used operationally by both the Spanish and Egyptian air forces.

HA 300

Messerschmitt completed his fighter-plans with the HA 300 in Egypt. This was his last personal development. The two-engined interceptor jet-fighter was begun at Hispano Aviation in 1953. A flying full-scale mock-up took to the air on 25 June 1959. As the "Orpheos" engine manufactured by Bristol was not available with an after-burner, the costs for the necessary plant were over budget and the USA was giving Spain military aid, in 1960 Spain abandoned the HA 300 development. The construction plans were then sold to Egypt. Messerschmitt and his colleagues developed three prototypes and Ferdinand Brandner the appropriate E-300 turbine. The maiden flight took place on 7 March 1964. The Egyptian project of its own interceptor fighter was given up in 1969 and bombers bought from the Soviet Union. Thus the prototypes HA 300 V-1 to V-3 were left. The

Aircraft Type:	HA 300 V-1 and V-2
Purpose:	Interceptor fighter
Crew:	One
Engine plant:	1 x Bristol "Orpheus" 703 (21.5 kN, 2200 hp)
Wingspan:	5.84 m
Length:	11.1 m
Height:	3.15 m
Wing area:	17.5 sq.m
Top speed:	2125 kms/hr
Cruising speed:	1550 kms hr
Landing speed and rate of climb:	Unknown
Weight empty:	3800 kgs
All-up weight:	5500 kgs
Service ceiling:	18000 m
Range:	1800 kms
Armament:	2 cannons

German engineers had to leave the country and the plan to market the HA 300 as a vertical take off aircraft came to nothing.

The aircraft was rejected by the Egyptian air force on the grounds of better value engine plants elswhere.

The Messerschmitt foundation has this well-restored HA 300 prototype.

Project 141

Project Me P 141 was planned as a "simple transport" for a payload of 3,500 kgs. The aircraft was a high-wing monoplane with two turbo-props to be built specially for regions without a developed road network. Loading and unloading would be done through two hinged doors. The easily maintained, fixed undercarriage would even have made possible landings on poor quality airfields. The project was first exhibited at the Paris Aérosalon in 1963. By equipping the machine with Rolls-Royce "Dart Mk 503E" it was thought possible to increase the payload to 9,200 kgs. A joint project with Portugal was concluded to build 100 transporters at Beja, but the financial arrangement broke down and put an end to this promising project. The further development of the P 142, an enlarged P 141, was envisaged as a simple passenger airliner for 37 persons for use particularly in Africa.

The project for a light transport aircraft Me P 141 was intended for the Third World.

Aircraft Type:	Project P 141
Purpose:	Transport aircraft
Crew:	Three
Engine plant:	2 x Turbomeca "Bastian"
Wingspan, length, height, wing area, service ceiling and rate of climb:	All unknown
Top speed:	610 kms/hr
Cruising speed:	480 kms/hr
Landing speed:	150 kms/hr
Weight empty:	4300 kgs
All-up weight:	7500 kgs
Range:	1000 kms

Project P 160 and SP 160

Messerschmitt project P 160 was intended to replace aircraft such as the Vickers Viscount 810 or the Convair 440. A total of 18 different versions were made available on offer to airlines. The design displayed at the Paris Aérosalon had three turbines at the rear of the machine, two laterally and a third integral to the rudder unit. Calculations indicated that the aircraft could accommodate 58 passengers or 5,500 kgs airfreight. Work was done on the project between 1962 and 1964 and also on the successor, SP 160, but was abandoned for lack of interest by the airline companies.

Aircraft Type:	Project P 160
Purpose:	Short-range passenger aircraft
Crew:	Four
Engine plant:	3 x General Electric CF 700
Wingspan:	18.5 m
Length:	22.5 m
Height:	Not known
Wing area:	47.6 sq.m
Top speed:	900 kms/hr
Cruising speed:	745 kms/hr
Landing speed, rate of climb and weight empty:	Unknown
All-up weight:	18.6 tonnes
Service ceiling:	11,000 m
Range:	1000 kms

The Me P 160 had a strikingly modern appearance but did not come to fruition.

Project 308 "Jet Taifun"

Aircraft Type:	Project P 308
Purpose:	Business and tourist aircraft
Crew:	Two
Engine plant:	2 x General Electric CJ 610-4 (each 10.7 kN, 1090 hp)
Wingspan:	9.75 m
Length:	9.7 m
Height:	Unknown
Wing area:	13.4 sq.m
Top speed:	800 kms/hr at 12,000 m
Cruising speed:	710 kms/hr
Landing speed:	185 kms/hr
Rate of climb and weight empty:	Unknown
All-up weight:	5380 kgs
Service ceiling:	12,000 m
Range:	3000 kms

The Messerschmitt P 308 was to be linked to the legendary "Taifun" as a business and tourist aircraft and would seek markets not only in Europe. The machine designated Me 308 "Jet Taifun" could be fitted with seats for up to ten passengers, but as a rule for six. The two-man crew would occupy a pressure cabin: two jet turbines, for example General Electric GJ 610-4, were planned. Apart from the business executive role, the development could also serve other segments of the market, for example as a light military communications and transport aircraft for up to 14 men, or as an ambulance aircraft with a two-man crew, a medical orderly with four patients supine and two seated. Messerschmitt also offered the "Jet Taifun" as NASARR-training machine and in a variant as a ground attack aircraft. A full scale mock-up of the fuselage of the P 308 was made and a 1:4 wind tunnel model. The development had progressed far when in the spring of 1965 it was halted in the face of more promising developments.

Messerschmitt's idea was to link the Me P 308 "Jet Taifun" to the Bf 108 and Me 208.

Project 2020 "Rotorjet"

The development of vertical take-off aircraft (VTOL) was pursued in the mid-1960s by all large nations with an interest in aviation. In this period of the Cold War and the threat of atomic warfare, the military infrastructure needed operational aircraft which could take off and land almost anywhere. One of the most comprehensive projects of the time was the Messerschmitt P 2020 "Rotorjet" project which was studied at the end of 1969 as a military variant of an airliner. In 1968 the development office had decided upon two Turboméca single-shaft, twin-cycle jet turbines. The new engines were tested in a wind tunnel and a rotor test-stand built. Practical testing continued into 1971 and was then suspended in favour of other projects. The feasibility of VTOL transport aircraft of that type was not disputed but proved so complicated that the helicopter was preferred.

Aircraft Type:	Project P 2020
Purpose:	VTOL transport aircraft
Crew:	3-4
Engine plant:	2 x General Electric GE 1 (61.7 kN, 6300 hp)
Wingspan:	23.32 m
Length:	21.46 m
Height:	8.5 m
Wing area:	68 sq.m
Top speed:	870 kms/hr
Cruising speed:	820 kms/hr
Landing speed:	Unknown
Rate of climb to 2000 m:	3.8 mins
Weight empty:	16470 kgs
All-up weight (STOL):	30 tonnes
Service ceiling:	11300 kgs
Range with 4 tonnes:	2170 kms

Project Me P 2020 was a vertical take-off transport aircraft for civilian and military use.

VJ-101 A to E

In the specification issued by the Federal German Defence Ministry on 2 November 1956 a fast interceptor-fighter was required. In view of the vulnerability of airstrips, short take-off (STOL) and vertical take-off (VTOL) aircraft were needed. In 1959 the Development Ring was set up in which Messerschmitt was also a member. Apart from the VJ 101 A (Heinkel), Messerschmitt had worked on the VJ 101 B to the stage of a full scale mock-up. The joint project then led to the design of the VJ 101 C with six swivel-mounted turbines. A swivel-stand and two prototypes ensued. The practical testing of the prototypes took place on a telescopic column at Manching. Of the greatest interest were the engine tests and to examine the reliability of equilibrium in hovering flight.

Aircraft Type:	VJ-101 C XI
Purpose:	Vertical take-off aircraft (experimental)
Crew:	One
Engine plant:	6 x Rolls-Royce RB 145 and RB 145R
Wingspan:	6.61 m
Length:	15.6 m
Height:	4.13 m
Wing area:	18.6 sq.m
Top speed:	1240 kms/hr at 6000 m altitude
Cruising and landing speeds rate of climb and Range:	Unknown
Weight empty:	4120 kgs
All-up weight:	6 tonnes
Service ceiling:	12,000+ m, no armament

Ground testing of the VJ-101 X-1 and X-2.

The first free flight of the VJ 101C X-1 took place on 10 April 1963. The first complete take-off and landing transition was achieved on 8 October 1963. The first flight through the sound barrier (Mach 1.04) of a VTOL aircraft succeeded on 29 July 1963. The machine was wrecked on 14 September 1964 as the result of ground crew error after 65 free flights. On 12 June 1965 the VJ 101 C X-2 flew. The development of the fighter-bomber VJ 101 D, a slightly modified C-variant, was not completed, and nor was the work on the VJ 101 E, amongst other reasons because of the introduction of foreign machines. Work on the development of the vertical take-off aircraft was terminated on 27 January 1971.

Head-on view of the VJ-101 with its engines in the horizontal position.

Display of a landing by the VJ 101 X-1 with parachute brake.